Tillies

Tillie and Henderson Shirt Factory

GUILDHALL PRESS

First published in March 2005

Guildhall Press, Unit 15, Ráth Mór Centre,
Bligh's Lane, Derry BT48 0LZ
T: (028) 7136 4413 F: (028) 7137 2949
info@ghpress.com www.ghpress.com

Cover photograph courtesy of the University of Ulster archives

Copyright © Patrick Durnin/Guildhall Press

The author asserts his moral rights in this work in
accordance with the Copyright, Designs and Patents Act 1988

ISBN 0 946451 85 0

A CIP record of this book is available from the British Library

We gratefully acknowledge the financial support of Derry City Council
under its Main Grant Programme, and The Honourable The Irish Society.

This project is supported by the European Union, administered by the
Local Strategy Partnership for the Derry City Council Area.

EU Programme
for Peace and Reconciliation
In Northern Ireland and the Border Regions of Ireland

LOCAL STRATEGY PARTNERSHIP
DERRY CITY COUNCIL AREA

DERRY CITY COUNCIL

THE HONOURABLE
THE IRISH SOCIETY

Front cover photograph

Some Tillie and Henderson workers posing on the iron steps into the
factory over Tillie's Brae.

1. Unknown
2. Annie Doyle
3. Dan McDaid
4. Nellie Graham
5. Mary Donaghy
6. Willie 'Ginger' Quinn
7. Unknown
8. Ruby Campbell
9. Phyllis Doherty
10. Rosie Kelly
11. Unknown
12. Pam Moran
13. Joan McKeegan
14. Peggy Cassidy
15. Mina McKeegan
16. Margaret Long
17. Annie McGuinness
18. Ms Callan
19. Unknown
20. Collette Scallon
21. May Long
22. Kathleen McCart
23. Unknown
24. Jenny Browne
25. Eileen Ryan

Acknowledgements

I am indebted to Professor Robert Gavin (retired Provost, University of Ulster) and Annesley Malley FRICS, MRAC, Chartered Surveyor, for their contribution to this publication. My sincere gratitude is expressed to Berna McDermott who performed the role of facilitator by organising evenings of reminiscence. Without these, and the contributions of the women who took part in them, there could not have been a genuine Tillie and Henderson story. To those women, and also to the other women who shared their memories with me on different occasions, I would like to express my gratitude.

I would particularly like to acknowledge Stella McDaid, Mary Lynch, Eithne Glackin, Phyllis McCourt, Mary McCloskey, May Lindsay, Anna Burns, Bridie Cooke, Sadie Morris and Roisin Gallagher. Special thanks to Margaret Mulheron for her encouragement.

My thanks are also extended to: Bill Quinn, Brian Nolan, Sammy Moore, Paddy McBay, Paddy Morrison, John Barber, Michael Lynch and John McCourt. Also to the staff of the Central Library Local History department for all their help and encouragement, in particular to Maura Craig. Special thanks to Julie A Grew for input from her M.Phil thesis *The Derry Shirt Making Industry, 1831-1913* published in 1987.

The photographs in the book came from the following sources: David Bigger (McDonald/Bigger collection), Joe McLaughlin, University of Ulster (Magee collection), Rose and Margaret O'Kane, George Sweeney, May Lindsay, Eithne Glackin, Mary Hegarty, Molly Martin, Stella McDaid, Hugh Gallagher, Bobby White, Peter McCarron, Margaret Mulheron and Derry City Council archivist Bernadette Walsh.

My appreciation to our funders, Derry City Council and The Honourable The Irish Society, and Paul Hippsley, Joe McAllister, Declan Carlin, Michael O'Hanlon and Aaron Murray of Guildhall Press.

Finally, within my own family environment I appreciate the patience and encouragement of my wife Mary, and children Louise, Ciaran, and Ronan.

Contents

*To the factory girls of Derry, and in particular,
those in Tillie and Henderson.*

Factory Girl

(Courtesy of Roy Arbuckle)

Horns blowing, so forlorn, dreary Derry dawn,
Head bent against the day, scarf and rollers on;
Hands tucked inside her sleeves, through the wind and rain,
And the Factory Girl goes off to work again.

There's Bridie and her sister, there's Mary and Siobhan,
And Maggie and wee Lizzie and Jinnie's husband John;
He's working in the cutting room along with Joe and Sam,
For men need work and the band knife needs a man.

Chorus
And oh! I love those factory girls,
Shirts they make are worn around the world,
In Paris and in London, Americay and Spain,
So the Factory Girl goes off to work again.

She's looking for Tony, he works down at the docks,
Well at least he goes there everyday, and sometimes he stops and talks;
And she likes the way he looks at her, but she'll never let him know,
For factory girls don't let their feelings show.

Her head is full of last night, the dancing and the crack,
And soon it will be Thursday, time for paying back;
The Credit Union loan is due, and the Provident's the same,
So the Factory Girl goes off to work again.

Horns blowing, so forlorn, dreary Derry dawn,
Head bent against the day, scarf and rollers on;
Hands tucked inside her sleeves, through the wind and rain,
And the Factory Girl goes off to work again.

About the Author

Patrick Durnin worked as a cutter in Tillie and Henderson shirt factory in Foyle Road during 1950-1972. He established the Waterside Local History Group in 1989 which was instrumental in protecting and preserving the old Derry workhouse in the Waterside from demolition. Patrick created further interest in the workhouse through his two previous publications, *Derry and the Irish Poor Law* published in 1991 and *The Famine and the Workhouse in Derry* (Guildhall Press, 2001). This latest publication, *Tillies*, describes what working 'beside the girls' was like.

Preface

After standing for one hundred and forty-seven years as a testament to the industrial achievement of William Tillie and a tribute to the sewing skills of the Derry factory girl, the derelict Tillie and Henderson building fell victim to vandalism and was ultimately demolished on 4 January 2003.

The building opened on 30 December 1856 and gave birth to the embryonic shirt trade that had already existed in the city. Its demolition was symbolic of the end of the entire city shirting industry, which has now all but passed into folklore. Affectionately known as 'Tillies', the factory was a familiar landmark on the Abercorn Road end of Craigavon Bridge and represented a substantial era in the city's social history. That history recorded the evolution of shirt making in the city from the hand-sewn shirt to the machine-stitched modern garment, from the fireside shirt-making tradition to a factory industry. It was an evolution that put Derry on the industrial map and transferred the role of breadwinner onto the women and girls in a city plagued with male unemployment.

Although this publication is specifically about Tillie and Henderson, it can also be seen as representing the story of all the city's shirt factories, for apart from some minor variations, shirt production and day-to-day life were similar in all the factories.

The History of the Clothing Industry in Derry was written by Professor Robert Gavin and first published in a slightly different form by Context Gallery in their magazine *Fabrics & Fabrication* in 2001. His meticulously researched work gives a knowledgeable, informative insight into this topic and relates the subsequent development, growth and decline of Derry's shirt industry.

The Historical Background to Tillie and Henderson was written by Annesley Malley, a much-respected researcher and local historian, who has served on a variety of public bodies and committees concerned with architectural and natural environments. It was adapted from his article, The Burning of Tillie and Henderson, first published in The Foyle Civic Trust Review 2002/2003. Mr Malley details the

William Tillie (1823-1904) in late 1890s when he was Lieutenant for the City of Londonderry. (Courtesy Ted McQuilken)

personal profile and industrial ingenuity of William Tillie, whose name was to become synonymous with shirt making in the city. His comprehensive account provides an appropriately historical beginning to the Tillie and Henderson narrative.

In the chapter on Shirt Production in Tillies, I draw from my own working experience as a cutter in Tillies, as well as from personal research, to show how the practical application of the developing technology and changing marketing and retailing techniques gave impetus to the production process.

Throughout the book, I have attempted to bring a sense of true-to-life realism to the Tillie and Henderson story through the reminiscences of former employees interviewed about their working lives in Tillies. There were remarkable similarities in their memories as they recalled and retold the social interaction of life in Tillies. Their contribution to the publication has been invaluable. Some of the people interviewed wished to remain anonymous. I have respected this request; it does not detract from the authenticity of their stories.

Approximately thirty-four tradesmen and apprentices also worked in Tillies, together with a factory manager, general manager and department managers. They, too, are an integral part of the story.

Patrick Durnin

History of the Clothing Industry in Derry

Professor Robert Gavin

Characteristics of the Industry

The clothing industry has a number of peculiar characteristics which differentiate it from many other forms of industrial manufacture and have affected the pace and direction of its development.

1. Unlike the metals and earths that are the raw materials for many other industries, the chief inputs to the clothing industry are relatively expensive fabrics that can represent up to 40% of the cost of the finished product and emanate in the main from relatively powerful supplier firms.

2. Fabrics are highly flexible materials varying in thickness and elasticity; the stitches that attach them are universal joints.

3. The movement of the material within the productive process is inherently unpredictable and difficult to control, requiring frequent exercise of human judgement.

4. Machining currently represents no more than 20% of the productive operation, the remainder representing various forms of material handling. The scope for automation is limited; consequently, production is labour intensive.

5. The end product has to be literally tailored to the individual needs of a wide variety of consumers and answer to their various tastes in terms of look, convenience and feel. To a greater or lesser extent it is collectivised by fashion, branding and other external influences on individual consumer demand. Marketing clothing product is neither simple nor inexpensive.

What is surprising, then, is not that the clothing industry moved rather more tardily and uncertainly along the path toward factory-based mass production than some of its confrères, but that it moved as quickly as it did.

Origin of the Derry Shirt Industry

The first great strides in this direction were taken in Derry in the middle years of the nineteenth century when Tillie and Henderson, McIntyre, Hogg and Marsh, Welch Margetson and others raised a ring of factories around the city walls, while a number of smaller concerns were ensconced within. These entrepreneurs had skilled stitchers to hand, for Derry's last linen weaver, William Scott, along with others from the city and elsewhere, had in the previous ten years been putting out large quantities of shirt-making and other sewing work to women in the city and the rural areas beyond. Using the product of local handloom weavers and bought-in cloth, William Scott, his son and others, could produce shirts at a rate approaching a quarter of a million shirts a year. But there was a world of difference between what Scott did and what happened in the new factories.

Factory Machining

The key new technology that Tillie and the other factory owners used was the sewing machine. It had just become sufficiently reliable for industrial use and was shortly to be proliferated by Singer's mass production methods. Tillie, however, gave this technology an additional twist – one that was to remain uncommon in the industry – by coupling the sewing machines to a steam engine through a complex array of driving shafts and pulleys installed in the factory he opened in Foyle Road in December 1856. Steam power also required the long work benches that remained characteristic of Derry shirt-factory machine-shop layouts until after the Second World War. With sewing machines and skilled machinists, the Derry shirt factories were able to pull the repetitive hem-stitching work out of London, which had been hitherto the chief centre of clothing manufacture in the United Kingdom. By 1871, 40% of the United Kingdom's installed sewing-machine capacity was in Derry, with London holding slightly less and other United Kingdom regions trailing far behind.

Cutting and Sizing Garments

The second major innovation was the development in the City Factory of the steam-powered band-cutting knife, which replaced scissors and permitted the cutting of seventy or more thicknesses of cloth. This went hand in hand with the introduction for the first time of the sizing of garments based on anthropometric studies in the United States that showed regularities in the human form.

Manufactured garments had hitherto been described as 'slops', which aptly described their fit, and sent all who could afford it to tailors or to their own households for the make-up of apparel. Within a few years, the Derry shirt makers were producing garments adapted to all customers and could equal the quality of London bespoke tailors at a considerably lower cost. Lay planning, marker making and cutting the relatively expensive fabric could make or break a manufacturer, and cutters (mostly male) became a class apart, paid at much higher rates than other workers.

As Marshall Tillie (son of firm-founder William Tillie) observed in 1912: "This process of marking out requires the utmost nicety and precision to avoid waste. In fact, so skilfully is this important work done that of a piece of cloth eighty yards long, scarcely enough waste remains to cover an eggcup."

One may doubt this claim, which exceeds the performance of a modern, skilled operator using computer-aided design, but Marshall Tillie's point about the key importance of the cutting function to the whole process of factory-based clothing production remains.

Many of the garments made up by Scott and his contemporaries in Derry were cut by clothing merchants based elsewhere and this remained an option for local manufacturers. The new Derry factory owners, however, cut their own cloth and therefore controlled design.

The Factory System

Indeed, the chief characteristic of Tillie and Henderson and the three or four other major shirt makers in Derry was that they were merchants as well as manufacturers, who vertically integrated the processes of clothing production from fabric purchase to wholesale warehousing and sale. They selected their fabrics from a range of suppliers, designed and cut their garments, hem-stitched them in their factories, put them out to five or six times as many workers in the neighbouring counties for more detailed stitching, and brought them back to the factories for final arrangement and despatch to their own warehouses in England and Scotland. Unlike their predecessors, they rigorously controlled outworking through paid inspectors rather than agents, supplied complete packages with instructions, and paid cash rather than offering payment on final sale of the garment. Their control of their own design destiny was to stand them in good stead when they faced serious competitive challenges during the 1870s.

The 1870s Crisis

In 1860, the Derry factories were producing at a rate approaching five million shirts a year. This rate of Derry production was scarcely to be exceeded until the Second World War. It was more than enough for the home market in the British Isles, which at the time counted no more than ten million adult males, many of whom still had their shirts made at home. The surplus product was exported to the world-wide destinations represented by the figures on the frontal of the City Factory in Queen Street, but particularly to the United States.

During the 1870s, the American market was largely closed by rising tariffs and the emergence of a powerful United States shirt-making industry helped by individual Derry emigrants, as, in a more formal way, the next large export market in Australia was to be closed some forty years later by Derry-led local industry. At the same time, at home, the London industry recovered on a basis completely different from the Derry factory system. There the industry was vertically dis-integrated into a multiplicity of small specialist 'sweatshops' equipped with treadle sewing machines, each exploiting cheap female labour with skills limited to the repetitive execution of single operations and passing on their product to the next specialist producer on the way to the merchanting warehouse. What this system lost in quality control, it gained in adaptation to cheap labour and space availability.

Labour Conditions and Constraints

To meet this situation, the Derry shirt industry had to reinvent itself. At first, it considered going downmarket with cheaper products but ran into resistance from the workforce. However many outworkers could be recruited in rural districts, the supply of female labour, and particularly skilled machinists, in the city was limited. This may have been one of the reasons why the working conditions set from the start by Tillie and others were so relatively favourable. The working day began at 8.00am rather than 6.00am as was commonly the case in factories at the time. The working week was fifty rather than the usual sixty hours. The factories were centrally heated and lit by gas. A doctor was in attendance. The steam-driven machines were as much to save worker effort as to ensure stitching regularity. Steam power entailed no substantial saving in cost. Social gatherings and outings were organised to encourage worker loyalty. That loyalty broke down in 1879 when Tillie, following the closure of the American market, proposed to manufacture cheaper products at a lower wage rate. The workers struck, despite Tillie's efforts to get their mothers to persuade them to work on. Windows were broken in another factory that proposed to take on Tillie's cheap work.

The 'White Shirt' Establishes Derry Shirt-Making Supremacy

Rebuffed by their workers, the Derry shirt makers devised a product that steered clear of worker opposition and capitalised upon the Derry industry's peculiar strength in quality mass production. This was the classic 'white shirt', a garment whose highly starched linen collar, breast and cuffs were adopted by the then emergent middle class as a uniform badge of rank to replace the ruffled, gophered and tucked finery that had previously adorned the 'gentleman's' throat, breast and wrists. During the 1880s, all the larger factories in Derry acquired state-of-the-art laundries and pressing rooms to finish their shirts in this way. Laundry workers were paid more than machinists, and rightly so. Despite many attempts, factories in England and in Europe were never able to match the 'Derry finish'. The Berlin, Celtic and other Derry-based brands had a quasi-monopoly of sales across the world outside the United States wherever men wished to be classified as 'white-collar workers'. Production of cheaper working men's shirts was left to English competitors, indeed was assigned to English factories owned by firms with plants in Derry. Derry settled down to producing between three and four million shirts a year, about 20% of United Kingdom production.

Market Turbulence and 'White Shirt' Decline

The relatively stable prosperity enjoyed by the Derry shirt industry during the last two decades of the nineteenth century gave way to serious turbulence in the first two decades of the twentieth century and severe shocks that altered the balance within the industry. Sharp price alterations in the cotton market in the first years of the century, and again at the end of the First World War, had a severe effect on sales, as did the dislocation brought about in 1914 by the onset of the war itself. This was reflected in the order books of one of the largest firms, McIntyre, Hogg and Marsh, which had accounted for 20% of the city's production at the end of the nineteenth century. Orders slid from a peak in excess of one million shirts in 1899 to less than half a million in 1906; rose, then dropped again from 600,000 in 1912 to 400,000 in 1914; rose once more to 600,000 in 1919, and dropped to less than 300,000 in 1920.

Not all firms were as badly affected. The majors like McIntyre, Hogg and Marsh, which merchanted material, suffered most from price fluctuations. Tillie and Henderson was ruined by price changes in 1920, and the original firm was forced to sell its plant in 1924. The majors were also most committed to the white-shirt business and this great staple of the industry began to go out of fashion between 1902 and 1912. White shirts accounted for 80% of McIntyre, Hogg and Marsh's production in 1903 and less than 24% in 1912.

Derry Factory Production at its Peak, 1914-1919

On the other hand, new firms were being created: in 1907, there were thirty firms in the city; in 1920, there were forty. The newcomers created new factory space. Sweeney erected a custom-built factory in

Foyle Street in 1914. The last great shirt factory on the Strand Road was built by Bryce and Weston at the end of the First World War. New factory space was needed. There had been two part-time out-workers for every factory worker in the first decade of the century. By 1919, virtually all production was concentrated in the factories. The outworkers' position had been eroded by faster and more specialised machines and the new fashion for simpler garments that did not need their detailed attention. Eventually, even at their lower wages, their product cost three times what the factories could produce.

The Derry factory workforce must have expanded to take up the strain, for the level of activity during the war years was very high. War Office orders for uniforms ran at a rate equal to some 46% of pre-war production while Derry retained most of its civilian markets. Trade to the distant colonies was lost but was compensated for by gains in Mediterranean and Scandinavian countries where German and Austrian competition was excluded by blockade.

Before the war, there had been some 5,000 workers, including laundry workers, in the Derry factories. During the war, numbers may well have surpassed the 6,000 mark, representing the highest level of clothing-industry employment ever to be experienced in the city.

Weaknesses in a One-Industry City 1920–39
After this last bout of prosperity came the lean, disappointing years of the interwar period. Much capacity lay idle; short-time working became common and unemployment more pervasive in the industry than at any time other than the difficult years of white-shirt transition between 1903 and 1911. Largely because other industry in the city suffered even worse, this was also the period when the shirt industry most completely dominated the city's economy. It employed more people than all of transport, commerce and distribution put together and sustained many jobs in each of these areas. The whole demographic pattern in the city was skewed toward the sustenance of the shirt industry's mainly female workforce. Much hinged on the industry's success. But leadership in the industry was faltering, uncertain and beset by nostalgia for past products and achievements.

Conservative Response to Challenges

There were major challenges to be faced. Overseas markets had been largely lost through the growth of local industry in the more distant outlets and sharply resurgent European competition in those nearer at hand, assisted by an absurdly high sterling exchange rate. In the home (British) market, competition now chiefly came from new factories nurtured by War Office orders during the war years rather than the London sweatshops that were going the way of Derry's outworkers.

Many of the new plants were based in the Lancashire textile districts and benefited from proximity to fabric producers, who at this time were driving the market with new poplin, cellular and other products. On the distribution side, powerful new department and chain stores were transforming the retail scene and displacing the multiplicity of gentlemen's outfitters with whom the Derry firms had traditionally done business. Squeezed between increasingly powerful suppliers on the one hand and retailing clients on the other, there was little room left for innovative design development and market making by the Derry producers. The bulk of the smaller firms were beholden to English merchant houses that provided them with fabric and finance and virtually controlled the fate even of some second-ranking firms. Even the Derry merchanting majors, which had lost much ground within the local industry, largely assigned control over marketing policy to their head offices and warehouses across the water.

Insofar as the Derry industry had a marketing stance, conservatism was the general rule. The majors clung as close to the top of the quality range as they dared, producing the 'fancy' shirts that replaced the white shirt. The smaller players produced further down the range as opportunity offered. All were more production plants than innovative manufacturers.

Forcing Wages Down

Collectively, their chief response to the new environment was to take advantage of a disastrous cutters' strike in the middle of the 1920s recession to impose through the Wages Board a 7% differential between the Derry wage and that in England. Hitherto, wage rates in the Derry factories had been higher than in England, an exceptional state of affairs that was justified by the strength of the city's competitive position. Now, it was argued, a differential was required to cover additional transport costs and permit effective competition with similar plants in Great Britain. Transport of goods, from fabric suppliers in Great Britain and back to retail markets there, was undoubtedly a competitive consideration. But no recorded costs justified the extent of the differential. Crushed by the failed strike, the Trade Union, which had no organiser in Derry from then until 1947, was in no position to argue the point. The policy endured up to and beyond the middle of the Second World War.

Transformations in the British Clothing Industry

While the Derry shirt industry was experiencing these travails, the clothing industry in Great Britain was going through a major transformation. It was one of the main beneficiaries of the growth of the electric power industry that was one of the main industrial hallmarks of this period, along with the proliferation of compact electrically driven devices. The potentiality of the new technology within the clothing industry was tapped by an outpouring of operational research on the costing of the various clothing operations, new ideas on factory layout and design and the deployment on shop floors of what were described as line-production methods. Across the industry, productivity doubled between the wars, chiefly by producing the same volume of product with fewer workers.

Tardy Adoption of New Methods in Derry

These changes came late to Derry. Whether because the industry in the city had already advanced so far along this path before 1920, or because its commitment to established technology was too great, or simply through lack of managerial capacity to invest and undertake the far-reaching changes required, the Derry firms did not adopt the new methods until around 1935 when they had become generalised elsewhere.

Another factor cannot be disregarded. With unemployment in the city at astronomical levels, there were no prizes for shedding labour in

Derry. And there was the cushion of the wage differential. Derry firms could continue to compete with more productive firms in England because Derry wages were lower. However this may be, productivity in the Derry industry, which probably rose substantially between 1910 and 1920, failed to rise between then and 1935. With the adoption of new systems, there was some improvement between 1935 and 1937, but the major leap forward took place during the Second World War.

Shirt Making under Government Control 1940–1950

The Second World War altered the whole context in which the Derry clothing industry operated for a period of over ten years. Armed Services orders, followed by the introduction of clothes rationing, sidelined suppliers and retailers and made the industry subject to government fibre and fabric quotas and the flows of military contracts and clothing coupons. Fashion and the vagaries of consumer taste were virtually abolished by the institution of the Utility scheme in 1942. This scheme also costed every production operation and left a profit margin that catered for all but the least efficient producers. This was a production manager's dream. War uniforms had laid the basis for factory production in other countries like the United States. Putting the whole civilian population in uniform provided the long runs and planning perspectives that could build great businesses.

Moreover, the British Government became anxious to transfer as much clothing production as possible to Northern Ireland, to clear the way for munitions production in Great Britain. One of the Derry industry's chief pre-war competitors, McArthur Beattie of Warrington, transferred the greater part of its production operation to Derry. Other British firms, however, were consolidated into highly efficient units that were to resume yet sharper competition at the end of the war. In these circumstances, the production-orientated Derry industry, with ample spare capacity and trained machinists to hand, was bound to prosper. Between 1937 and the end of the war, Derry productivity practically doubled and production volume reached unprecedented heights.

Missed Opportunities

The Second World War, however, did not yield the same jobs bonanza as the first. Despite total war mobilisation, employment in the Derry clothing industry was the same 6,000 at the end of the war as it had been in July 1940 and was always below that figure in the intervening years. The workforce had grown more substantially in the difficult times between 1924 and 1937. The reason for this was that the Belfast Department of Commerce had other priorities. In the early years of the war, it diverted Armed Services shirt contracts to the linen industry in the south east of the Province, stricken by shortage of flax. When munitions production got under way in Belfast and diverted stitchers from the labour market there, the department erroneously assumed there was a shortage of stitchers in Derry, too. Efforts were made to direct production to rural areas, and desperate requests from London that Northern Ireland take on more clothing work were rebuffed while Derry stitchers stood on dole queues.

The Derry industry was rather smaller at the end of the war than it might have been, and that counted in the battle for quotas that continued until the Utility scheme was phased out. But wartime factory reorganisation left the reduced number of Derry firms in better shape to face post-control competition. Derry productivity was about 10% lower than the average of the streamlined industry in Great Britain, but 20% higher than the rest of Northern Ireland.

Raising Productivity and Shedding Jobs

The momentum of technological change was maintained in the post-war years, as it had to be to keep a step ahead of increasingly threatening competition from other producers at home and abroad. New equipment was brought in, much of it initially from the United States where major advances had taken place that could not properly be tapped until sufficient dollar currency was available. With the equipment came expertise. American and other consultants were employed to reassess factory layouts, introduce work-study methods, and make best use of new plant. Formal training began in factories, almost for the first time. Skills had previously been passed on by forms of apprenticeship through the dense informal networks that had grown up within the industry and in the community beyond.

Many of these changes involved shedding labour, for the city's share of the UK market remained fairly constant at a volume of around five million shirts per annum. Northern Ireland's share of the UK market had risen substantially since pre-war days. In the 1930s, it had fallen as low as 16%; in the 1950s, it ran closer to 25%. But Derry's share of the Northern Ireland share had steadily fallen from 72% before the war, to just over 60% in the war years and fell again in the 1960s to below 50%. Government policy to promote dispersal of the industry, conceived during the war, was having its effect. Derry's shirt-making workforce declined gently from over 5,000 in the 1950s, to something over 4,000 in the late 1960s and then slid heavily in the following decade to little over half that number, though this was increasingly compensated for by a shift to the manufacture of other clothing products.

The Demise of Bulk Shirts Production
During the shirt-industry crisis of the 1970s, many of the old firms associated with the industry since it started were wiped from the slate. Some went into liquidation; some were the subject of management buyouts. Most were taken over and amalgamated by what eventually became the great British clothing combine, Coates Viyella, which continued the bulk shirts business on a much smaller basis than before, employing around 1,000 workers. These were accommodated at Trench Road and Campsie on the city outskirts to which the industry largely migrated, abandoning the old shirt factories that had been systematically established in the most populous residential areas to reduce distances to work. In this period, the Derry shirt industry took a severe knock, much more severe than across Northern Ireland, where only 20% of jobs were shed. New manufacturers appeared upon the scene to take advantage of skilled labour, but they too, along with Coates Viyella's shirt-making operation, survived only to the end of the century. Bulk shirt production could not compete in the new environment; and the field was left to smaller specialist shirt manufacturers like Graham Hunter, producing for niche markets.

Other Branches of Clothing Manufacture

The Derry clothing industry had never been exclusively devoted to shirt making. Throughout the second half of the nineteenth century and most of the twentieth century, there had always been a small accompanying commitment to ladies' and men's underwear, night-wear and other articles. The prominently placed Star Factory was originally built in 1900 by Bayer's of London for the production of ladies' underwear. This, however, was exceptional and short lived. Other clothing production was mainly carried out in small depart-ments run by the shirt-making majors. It was regarded as a hedge against vicissitudes in the shirt trade and was liable to be crowded out when the main business was going well.

The volume of other clothing production in the city at the begin-ning of the twentieth century reached up to 20% of shirt-making vol-umes. But in general, it was much lower and probably engaged no more than 10% of the workforce. Across Northern Ireland, more or less half the clothing workforce was assigned to the shirt-production category throughout the twentieth century, which compared with substantially less than 20% in the United Kingdom as a whole.

The Nature of the 1970s' Crisis

Shirt making had ruled the roost in Northern Ireland because the rel-ative regularity and predictability of production in this field was suit-ed to large-scale plants like those in Derry, operating at a distance from the points of sale. The progressive withdrawal of government protec-tion from the British clothing market and its exposure to competition from rising low-cost producers, first in Europe, then in Africa and Asia, turned Derry shirt-making strengths into weaknesses. To survive, Derry had to act like a local near-market supplier to differentiate itself from menacingly cheap, more distant producers. A radical re-think of strategy was required, much as had been the case almost exactly 100 years before. The conventional wisdom that preferred long runs to areas of greater market volatility had to be set aside. The needs of the market had to be re-addressed. More attention had to be paid to the finishing end of the business and the interface with retail outlets.

The Desmond Response: Market Interface

The foremost practitioner in these new arts was Denis Desmond, who took control of his family's business in 1972. Desmonds had been a small player on the Derry scene since the late nineteenth century, establishing a specialism in pyjama manufacture since 1924 when, with the Derry shirt majors, it promoted an exhibition for the sale of that product. In the 1970s, demand for pyjamas was relatively buoyant.

More importantly, Desmonds had a long-standing connection with the rising High Street retailer, Marks and Spencer. Denis Desmond cultivated this connection, which developed into an almost symbiotic relationship, giving the firm's production plants access to immediate information on the movements of goods across retail counters. Production response to these movements was developed by the application of information-technology methods throughout the production process, centring on the automated warehouse in Drumahoe, where goods stands replicated those in Marks and Spencer's shopping malls. 'Just in time' became the order of the day and Desmonds claimed to deliver faster than plants in England. The distance bugbear, which had exercised shirt-making minds so greatly in 1920, had been scotched.

Diversifying Production

Desmonds also operated more freely across the market range than other firms, matching production capacity with market opportunity. Initially, pyjamas were the main product; twenty years later, they accounted for only 20% of production. With new investment and frequent staff re-training, production was moved to leisure wear, jeans and other articles as market opportunity offered. The jeans market in particular was consolidated by investment in finishing technology that few could match, echoing what had been done so long before with the white-shirt laundries. By the mid-1990s, Desmonds had over 3,000 workers, two-thirds as many as the shirt factories had generally employed throughout the previous hundred years. Not all were in Derry. Desmonds' plants were distributed across the west of Northern Ireland. But the bulk of employment was in the city and its environs, and the headquarters was in Drumahoe. But once again, low-cost overseas competition took its toll and, regrettably, Desmonds' last remaining operation at Drumahoe is scheduled to cease production in December 2005.

What the Future May Hold

The clothing industry is once more in travail. The multi-fibre arrangement which protected European markets is being phased out and low-cost overseas production must become an increasingly important factor in the equation for all those concerned with the transformation of fabrics into apparel for delivery to appreciative customers. Already, job losses in the industry in Derry and in Northern Ireland have been occurring at a faster rate than at any time in the past and there may be more to come.

But this is both a resilient and highly complex industry, comprising a multiplicity of operations. Even in simpler, nineteenth-century days, a substantial proportion of employment in the industry, much of it relatively better paid, was to be found in the warehousing, finishing, marketing and design sections of the industry. These functions, along with prototyping and the specialist and niche-market production that support them, are relatively immune from overseas competition. Happily, Derry has acquired a very firm footing in these fields. With good management, that foothold can be extended, the tradition of clothing manufacture in the city can be maintained, and a new period of better-founded prosperity can open up.

Historical Background to Tillie and Henderson

Annesley Malley

Established in 1851, in the wake of the Great Famine, the firm of Tillie and Henderson became one of the great manufacturing success stories of the north of Ireland. For more than a century, the headquarters of the firm, the Foyle Factory in Londonderry, was the hub of a shirt-making empire which exported its wares throughout the world. Its founding partners were William Tillie and John Henderson – who gave the firm its name – and Robert Sinclair from the manufacturing business of Sinclair's in Glasgow, who had previously employed Tillie as an agent.

The three partners had all the expertise required for a successful business. Henderson controlled the Glasgow warehouse and looked after the marketing, later moving to the London branch when Sinclair left the partnership in 1862. As an established manufacturer, Sinclair had a ready-made distribution network. William Tillie, through his work for Sinclair's, had local knowledge about the trade; it was his vision, entrepreneurship and philanthropy which were to be the driving forces behind the success of the firm.

Born in 1823 in Crookston Mains in Midlothian, Scotland, William was the son of John Tillie of Torwood Lee, a small village in the Melrose area. Little is known of William Tillie's early life or education. As an employee of Sinclair's of Glasgow, he was frequently in Derry in connection with the shirt-making business, although at this time the industry was only in its early infancy in Derry, William Scott and Richard Gibbons having in 1849 set up as agents, receiving ready-cut shirts from English and Scottish houses and employing seamstresses to make the shirts which were then shipped back. Recognising the business potential offered by the large labour pool available, not only in the city itself, but in the surrounding districts, Tillie persuaded Henderson and Sinclair to join him in setting up a factory in Derry in which the shirts would be cut out and distributed to local stations where the workers could collect bundles of unmade shirts. When the bundles of shirts were returned to the factory, they would be sorted and packed, ready for export, thereby cutting out the middlemen in a much more cost-effective exercise. In this way, Tillie and Henderson would change production in Derry from a cottage industry into a highly centralised factory process, a change which was welcomed in the local press:

In addition to providing secure employment, its advantages will be all the more felt, as, by the fact that Messrs Tillie and Henderson employ all the workers directly, the latter are preserved from those annoyances inseparable from the 'middleman' system which formerly prevailed.

In 1851, then, Tillie, together with his new bride, Agnes Marshall Lee, came to Derry to set up this innovative enterprise, settling in Bellview House in the Waterside area of the city.

With an initial staff of forty workers, the firm obtained premises in Little James Street and had local stations in Claudy, Donemana, Strabane, Newtownstewart and throughout Inishowen in County Donegal.

From the beginning, the company prospered. But the real expansion in the firm began when, in 1852, Tillie became the first manufacturer to introduce the sewing machine to Derry. Having seen the machine for the first time in Edinburgh, Tillie was quick to recognise its revolutionary nature and quickly sought out the London agents for the Thomas sewing machine, ordering 100 machines, for which he paid £2,100. The business was removed to more commodious premises in Foyle Street, which lay close to the present Guildhall, to accommodate the new machines. An article on the growth of the shirt trade published in the *Derry Journal* on 21 October 1912 gives a first-hand account of the introduction of the sewing-machine:

The machine was made by Grover and Baker. It had two needles; one passing through the goods and the other operating beneath the cloth. It made as much noise as, and very similar to, a present-day motor bicycle, and was only fit to make up coarse working-men's shirts. As

with all introductions of labour-saving machinery, there was consid-
erable opposition by the hand workers.

Despite this opposition, the expansion of the firm was phenomenal and, by 1856, a decision was taken to build a new factory.

The new factory building at the corner of the original Wapping Lane and Foyle Road (Abercorn Road not being constructed until after 1863) was probably designed by a local architect, John Guy Ferguson, and built by W & A McIlwee. It was an 'L' shaped, red-brick building, covering an area of 19,000 square feet and stood four stories high. The cost of the building was £7,000, and when it was opened on 30 December 1856, after having been under construction for only five months, it was the largest manufacturing unit in Derry. The Foyle Factory was heated by the steam pipes that drove the new treadle Grover and Baker sewing machines, and was the first factory in Derry to use such innovative machinery. It started production with 450 workers, although in total, Tillie and Henderson employed some 4,000 workers at this time. An article in the *Derry Journal* on 23 March 1860 describes the layout and working life of the Foyle Factory:

Each floor is thrown into a single room and in these rooms are hundreds upon hundreds of busy workers, cutters, sewers, machine workers, clerks, and superintendents. Everyone has his or her own work defined, and this must be done, and well done. The sewing machines, which stand in rows, are driven by steam, and tended by girls of various ages, from the child of ten to twelve to the grown woman.

It also a sign of William Tillie's ingenuity and business acumen that in October 1859 he patented an improvement to the sewing machines which could be applied to models driven by hand, foot or steam. The invention was a clamping guide for directing the machines. As the same article went on to report:

Mr Tillie has patented an improvement of his own in these machines – a contrivance by which they are rendered self-acting, a girl being able to attend several of them at once.

Despite such labour-saving improvements, such was the demand for shirts at the time that the labour force also rapidly increased and, by 1862, the firm employed 800 people in the factory. Small wonder, then, that the premises, which at first seemed to be generously designed, soon proved too small, and large extensions became necessary from time to time. In 1862, a separate factory was built on a site between Ferguson's Lane and Bennett's Street. This was another large building of four stories with a large glass-roofed room attached where the machines could work. This building was apparently erected in thirty-six days, and with the increased space Tillie's workforce rose to 1,300 factory workers.

Also in 1862, Robert Sinclair left the firm by amicable agreement and built the Abercorn Factory on the corner of Abercorn Road and Wapping Lane which employed 1,200 workers. This competition seems to have had little effect on the meteoric success of Tillie and Henderson, as by 1866, a further expansion was called for and a distinctive 'frontal' block, designed by John Guy Ferguson, was added. The design was in a French château style and was angled to suit the gap between the existing factory and the new Carlisle Bridge completed in 1863.

This expansion gave Tillie space to exercise his philanthropic nature. He opened a school for his employees, mainly for girls under the age of fifteen, in one of the attic rooms in the new mansard roof. The school was partly funded by a grant from the Commissioners of National Education and functioned until 1876, and with the glut of new factories in the city, it proved a shrewd way of attracting and training workers. Limited housing was also constructed by the company along Foyle Road in this period.

The working conditions in the Foyle Factory brought it to the attention of Karl Marx and impressed him so much that he cites it as an example of good practice in *Das Kapital*. The Marx connection was reinforced when his daughter, Dr Eleanor Aveling, visited the factory in 1891, though at this time she was publicly critical of the low wages paid to the women in the factory and the practice of making them pay for anything that went wrong with the machines. Following

Carlisle Bridge, c1865, and to the left, the original Tillie and Henderson factory before the Abercorn Road extension. (Courtesy WELB collection)

publication of Dr Aveling's speech, heated denials were printed by the local press, including an interview with Tillie and Henderson workers who refuted her allegations.

By 1898, the factory had expanded again. A fifth floor was added to the original wing in Foyle Road and a new laundry was built on the Abercorn Road side of the factory. Again, the extension was designed by John Guy Ferguson and increased the size of Foyle Factory to 21,000 square feet. The total workforce employed in the Foyle Factory at this time was over 4,500, the vast majority of which were women. The firm also employed another 2,000 women at the outworkers' stations. At the turn of the century, shirt making was the largest industry in Derry with thirty factories exporting their goods to all corners of the world.

The Foyle Factory was not only the largest shirt-making factory in Ireland, it was the largest in the world. John Henderson had retired some fifteen years earlier, but the firm still retained his name, and his place had been filled by Marshall Tillie, William's third son.

The new century heralded the passing of an era for the Tillie family on a personal level, with the death on 4 September 1900 of Agnes Marshall Lee Tillie at Duncreggan, the house designed for the family by John Guy Ferguson in 1863 and now part of the junior school of Foyle and Londonderry College. A few years later, on 8 March 1904, following a short illness, William Tillie, aged eighty-one, also passed away at Duncreggan. Despite a slight deafness in his later years, he continued an interest in the firm and carried out his duties as His Majesty's City Lieutenant, to which he was appointed by Queen Victoria in 1898, until two weeks prior to his demise. The couple were survived by a family of five sons and three daughters. In his will, William Tillie left a fortune of £196,880, a measure of the success of the firm he founded; but both of them also left behind a legacy of charitable and civic works which showed that it was not only through the business that they had made their mark on the city of Derry.

William Tillie brought with him from Scotland a firm Presbyterian faith. Throughout his life, he was an elder of First Derry Presbyterian Church, contributing generously to its building funds and donating two commemorative windows; one to his late son-in-law, Rev Dr A C Murphy, who had been a former minister of the church. He was also a generous supporter of the Presbyterian Church in Ireland and was one of the wealthy laymen who, at the time of the Disestablishment of the Irish Church in 1869 and the abolition of Regium Donum, pledged to subscribe annually to the Sustentation Fund to prevent the ministry sustaining any loss from the changes. He also donated £500 to the Twentieth-Century Fund of the Presbyterian Church.

His charitable interests tended to centre on the education and the welfare of the families of the ministers, possibly due to the fact that his second daughter was the widow of a clergyman. This concern led him to contribute generously towards the erection of First Derry

School on Mall Wall, to the erection of houses for the professors of Magee College, and many smaller tokens to individual ministers' families. Agnes Tillie also involved herself in charitable enterprises, chief of which was her interest in providing nursing for the working classes. As Vice-President and founding member of the Londonderry District Nursing Society, she personally financed a fully equipped District Nurses' Home in Great James Street.

As well as his Church interests, William Tillie was involved in the political life of the city. Initially a committed Liberal, he supported Gladstone's candidates, but with the Home Rule question he declared for the Union and helped to organise the Ulster Convention. He was also appointed president of the Londonderry Unionist Association and lobbied energetically for the defeat of the Home Rule Bill.

For many years, he was a Grand Juror and a magistrate for both city and county. Although not a member of the Corporation, he occupied a seat at the Harbour Board. He was also a member of the Governing Body of Foyle College, where his sons were educated, and of the Committee of Administration of the Infirmary and the Asylum. He was a chairman of the Gaslight Company and a director to the Northern Counties Railway until it was amalgamated with the Midland Company. He was also a Bridge Commissioner. His memberships included the Gwyn's and Young's Board and the Chamber of Commerce. At the time of his death, he was His Majesty's Lieutenant for the City of Londonderry and Deputy Lieutenant for the county of Londonderry.

Following William's death, the Foyle Factory was managed by Marshall Tillie, who had been born at Bellview on 11 December 1857, his twin brother Alexander having been born the previous evening. Both boys were educated at Foyle College, but while Alexander received his further education in Glasgow, Marshall went to the International College in Paris.

Marshall married Mary Walker, the eldest daughter of a local merchant, and followed his father in becoming Deputy Lieutenant for the county of Londonderry and a member of many local boards. He was Mayor of Londonderry at the time of his father's death.

Marshall's eldest brother, William J Tillie, managed the Glasgow branch of the firm; however, he was often in poor health.

Alexander Tillie established a linen-manufacturing firm in Belfast, although he was resident permanently in London and was a member of the City of London Corporation. Deputy-Governor of The Honourable The Irish Society, he was also Chairman of the Guildhall School of Music and a Freeman of the City of London.

Another brother, Arthur, was the head of a large type-founding firm in London and the youngest, Charles R Tillie, was a solicitor in Londonderry.

Under Marshall's management, Tillie and Henderson continued to prosper. Like his father, he was keen to ensure that the machinery in the factory worked to its utmost efficiency. In 1908, he patented a collar-buttoning machine which reduced, by 50%, the thread used in this process. There was little in the way of building expansion, the only change being the addition in 1911 of an outside metal staircase onto Carlisle Square. However, in 1912, Tillie and Henderson purchased Sinclair and Company's Abercorn Factory, which could accommodate a further 1,200 workers and therefore could permit the firm to deal with the increased demand.

At the outset of the First World War, William J Tillie returned to the city to take over the management of the business, as his brother had to go abroad due to illness. Shortly following his return to the city in August 1915, Marshall died at Duncreggan, aged fifty-seven. As Marshall's only son had died young, William continued to look after the business until it went out of the family's control in 1928. The firm of Tillie and Henderson continued until the 1970s, when it closed its doors for the last time.

Shirt Production in Tillies

Having been the first to introduce the sewing machine into a factory setting in 1852, William Tillie exploited its production potential by connecting it to a steam engine through a system of shafts and overhead pulleys. In practice, the overhead pulleys with their large belts were connected to and rotated the long shafts on which were attached the smaller, fragile individual machine belts that activated the sewing-machine needle. Though the grinding mechanism of the system was located on the outside of the building, the overhead pulleys inside – with their constantly rotating and flapping canvas belts – created an ugly, unsightly, and at times noisy working environment. Indeed, the particular sewing machine, a Grover and Baker model that Tillie brought with him on the boat from Scotland, was both crude and noisy in itself.

This very basic machine could not do the finer and intricate stitching necessary to finish the shirts, which still had to be given to outworkers for completion. The combination hand-sewn and machine-sewn shirts were of the highest quality, and within a short time from the opening of the Foyle Road Factory, they gained a prize medal at the London exhibition of 1862. Despite its limited capabilities, the steam-driven sewing machine had the advantage to the girls that they didn't have to endure the pain and tiredness of working treadle machines with toe and heel.

At the time, there were other comparative advantages of working in Tillie and Henderson. Starting time was 8.00am, as against 6.00am in other factories, and the working week was fifty hours; the norm was sixty hours. Also, social outings and cultural activities were promoted, and quite successfully, in respect of the company choir, which had won the Hugh Stevenson Shield (sponsored by a large local bread manufacturer) outright at the local Feis Cheoil after having won the competition three years in succession, 1902-04. Unfortunately, research cannot reveal any further information about the choir except that the conductor was a Mr Anderson, and though the choir was ultimately disbanded, singing in the shirt factories among the girls remained an important characteristic of factory life.

Tillies' workers are the best singers. The shield presented by Messrs Hugh
Stevenson and Company for the factory competition at the local Feis
Cheoil and won outright by the Tillie and Henderson choir in 1904.

The cultural activity of the workers increased with the inclusion of a factory library, which aimed to promote and encourage loyalty to the firm, this in turn, hopefully, benefiting production output.

Better conditions were introduced for the welfare of sick and weakly workers. For example, they could be entitled to a holiday for their health in the seaside resort of Rathmullan in Co Donegal, which was financed by a levy imposed on those girls who were late for work in the mornings.

In the cutting room, where shirt production began, no cutting technology as such existed in the early years and working practices were tedious, monotonous and hazardous. The shirt pattern would be marked out on a single piece of cloth; this top cloth, as it was called, would be spread on the cutting table. Its length would be marked between two large pins that were fixed into holes which were drilled into an iron-edging bar on the table. Then several similar pins would be placed between these end-pins into similar holes and the cloth would be hooked onto the pins until the required amount of 'plies', or layers, were pinned. The hooked cloth would then be lifted onto the table by 'all hands'; and when the top cloth was placed on top of the hooked material, the cutters would proceed to cut out the shirt, using large sharp scissors and hand knives that left blisters and cuts on the their hands. However, help was to hand for the cutting operation and the steam-driven cutting knife made its appearance, greatly reducing the dependence on scissors and hand knives. The introduction of the band knife had a major impact on production:

The advent of steam was the forerunner of greatly improved methods in cutting. Hitherto, the cutting was done by hand, but with the new power, circular band knives were introduced, which cut material accurately to a depth of ten to twelve dozens.
(Mr G Morrish, *Londonderry Sentinel*, 19 October 1912)

It was in the City Factory that the band knife, as it was called, first made its appearance, the invention of that factory's superintendent mechanic, William Croom. Basically, the construction of the knife involved a very thin, pliable and sharp-edged steel band rotating

Smartly dressed female workers leaving Tillies in 1920s. (Courtesy David Bigger collection)

around three large wheels, two of which were below the work table of the knife and one above head height. The entire knife was enclosed by a wooden frame, except for about six inches of naked and unguarded blade for the actual cutting of the cloth. This cutting edge was sharpened by the operator, using two hand-held sandstones and then waxed with a candle that acted as a sort of lubricant. As a consequence of the new cutting technology, the 'hooking' system was seen as inadequate to exploit the cutting capacity of the band knife. So, the wooden cart, or cloth transporter as some would call it, for spreading the cloth on the table also made its appearance.

The cart was a simple wooden construction and was pushed along the top of the table with the operator, generally a female, pulling the cloth off while a second woman followed, spreading the material and keeping it straight and even on the table. When working the cart, the procedure was the same as before. The top marker cloth was placed on the table as usual and the determined length marked by two flat iron bars, similar to a yardstick, at each end. These were kept from moving by being placed between two large nails hammered into the table. As the cart passed the bars, the cutter would pull out the bar and the cloth would fold around it. The bar was then returned and the cart went down the table again. This was repeated until the required amount of plies were reached, then the top cloth was placed on, ready for cutting. By this time, around 1907, technology and the arrival of electricity produced a smaller mobile knife that was used for cutting the lay on the table into manageable blocks for the band-knife man to complete the cutting operation.

Around the same time of these improvements in the cutting department, it would appear that Marshall Tillie inherited his father's inventive nature when he was accredited with inventing a collar-buttonholing machine. Previously, the worker could only make one buttonhole at a time, but with the use of this new method, the worker was capable of operating three machines simultaneously. Both ends and the centre of the collar could now be buttonholed in less than three seconds. By comparison, the same labour and time that previously buttonholed thirty-four dozen now could buttonhole 396 dozen. Production was to further increase with the development of

A typical cutting-room scene. The 'hooking up' of the shirts. Notice pins on table edge, shirt patterns hanging on wall and 'twin' band knives. (Courtesy David Bigger collection)

the twin-needle machine, capable of 8,000 stitches per minute, double that of the single-needle machine. Not surprisingly, by the end of the first decade of the twentieth century, the majority of the 1,000 machines operating in Tillie and Henderson were electrically driven twin needles.

With such technological advances and the addition of a laundry and finishing department within the building, there was no further need for outworkers, and the weekly production, totalling 1,500 dozen shirts and 10,000 dozen collars, was now entirely factory-based. With the potential for production improving, it appeared that the working conditions of the women were deteriorating, according to the reports of factory inspectors. Commissioned under government factory legislation, inspectors were brought in to ensure that there was adequate ventilation, lighting, and heating within factories. In May 1908, they prosecuted Tillie and Henderson for not providing adequate heating in one of their departments, resulting in the women having to wear their hats, coats and scarves. The case was dismissed on a point of law.

In those early years, shirt production in Tillie and Henderson and in Derry's other large factories far exceeded demand in the home markets. As a result of this surplus, a booming export trade developed for the Derry-made shirt, mainly in the larger Australian, South African and American markets. American studies and research into the human anatomy established a sizing system that was to revolutionise not only the shirt trade but also the clothing trade in general. Factory shirts could now be manufactured that would conform to most shapes and sizes of the human body. They were now closer to tailor-made shirts and quickly became the choice of the well-dressed man. As a result of sizing, the shirt now had more component parts: collar, neckband, cuff, front and back bodies, yokes, and sleeves; these all extended over a large range of standard sizes. This was to radically alter cutting-room production practices and procedures, particularly in regards to cloth utilisation.

With a range of different shirt sizes and their various component parts, the marking out of the top cloth, or lay planning as it was later to be called, became more detailed and complicated. A greater degree of skill was now required from the lay planner when marking out the top cloth in order to achieve the maximum cloth utilisation.

Unfortunately, the virtual monopoly of the Derry-made shirt was not to last. Soon, the industry was faced with a major recession. Production dropped after the loss of the lucrative export markets. This had come about with the emergence in those countries of their own shirt industry and the rising tariffs on imported goods. Also, the English shirt industry re-invented itself with the production of coloured, cheaper working-men's shirts to replace the then almost standard white shirt. Faced with competition from the low-cost shirt on the home market, most of Derry's large factories decided to follow the trend of the different-coloured cheap shirt, as their very survival was threatened. To produce a low-cost garment required reducing production costs. In Tillie and Henderson, this met with determined opposition when, in November 1907, thirty-six machinists went on strike over the decision of the firm to reduce the rate of pay on certain classes of goods.

The dispute intensified as a result of the intransigence of Marshall Tillie, who took over management of the Derry factory after the death of his father in 1904. Tillie refused either to meet with a deputation of the girls or agree to arbitration. He further escalated the situation by advising those workers who did not accept the cost-cutting measures to leave and he immediately placed an advertisement in the local papers for replacement workers. The iron-fist approach brought strong condemnation from the Derry Trades Council, and after four weeks of negotiation, compromise was reached. The strike ended with the company agreeing to reduce the original pay-cut by half. Though the strike was damaging, trade-union militancy was not a characteristic of the shirt workers in those early years and not a serious impediment to production. The reason for this was that the women, who were the main wage earners supporting the family unit, did not feel they could afford to lose any wages.

In May 1908, Tillie and Henderson was registered and confirmed as a limited company with a share capital of £160,000. The official seal of the company incorporated the trade mark 'The Celtic'. (There has been persistent folklore that at one time the famous Glasgow Celtic Football Club had to seek permission to use the logo 'The Celtic'. Most probably the similarity was a coincidence.) There were five directors of the new company:

[signature]

David Sinclair – linen merchant and shirt manufacturer, London.

[signature]

Thomas MacFarlane – linen merchant and shirt manufacturer, Glasgow.

[signature]

William John Tillie – linen merchant and shirt manufacturer, Glasgow.

[signature]

Marshall Tillie – linen merchant and shirt manufacturer, Londonderry.

[signature]

Henry David Sinclair – linen merchant and shirt manufacturer, London.

The diversity and geographic spread of the of the directors indicated the 'all through' approach to shirt production, for Tillie selected and purchased his own material, designed his garments and stockpiled them in large warehouses in Scotland and England for bulk selling.

Tillie and Henderson official seal. Written on the crossbar of the monogram in the centre are the words 'The Celtic' and also two images of the 'Thistle', which symbolises the Scottish/Irish connection. (Courtesy Derry City Council archivist)

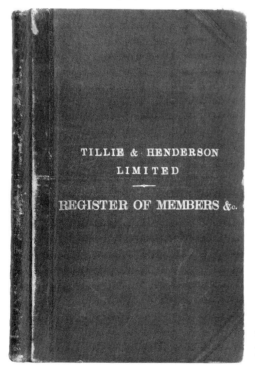

Tillie and Henderson Register of Members.

Cutting-room production stops for photo in early 1930s. In the suit is Davy Neely (production manager) and immediately beside him is Willie 'Ginger' Quinn. Wearing the apron is Jack Anthony. Also included are: Annie Donnelly, Nellie Graham, Tom McDaid (foreman cutter), Dan McDaid, Joe Callan, Alex Moore and Davy Knox. (Courtesy David Bigger collection)

While still producing the cheaper shirt, Tillie and Henderson, like other Derry factories, concentrated on the alternate strategy of producing a more expensive, up-market white shirt. With its smart and attractive finish of starched detached collar, cuffs and breast piece, the white shirt became associated with the professional worker and gave birth to the sociological term 'white-collar worker'. Helped by the First World War and the popularity of the up-market white shirt, production figures remained high right up to 1920, when the world price of cotton escalated and severely affected all the Derry shirt factories. This was followed in that same year by a recession in the trade and a prolonged strike by all the city's cutters in the middle of June.

After futile negotiations with the striking cutters, who were claiming a wage increase that would give them parity with English and Scottish shirt cutters, the Shirt Manufacturers Federation took advantage of the slump in sales and closed all the city's factories on Saturday 17 July to beat the strike. Also, a few of the city's manufacturers 'auctioned off' some of their orders to other factories in England and Scotland to fulfil contracts. Other customers were prepared to await delivery of their orders until a settlement was reached, as was the situation with Tillie and Henderson, which had been closed for eight weeks.

Eventually, a settlement was reached. The cutters reluctantly accepted a small increase in wages to avoid further hardship for the girls who had been living off a public subscription list during the closure. The factories re-opened on 25 August. These events (and the adverse trading situation that was to last longer than the cutters' strike) were to seriously affect the future of the Tillie and Henderson (1908) Company.

By April 1921 the company had been working on an overdraft of £40,000 and meetings between the members and the Bank of Scotland were taking place. That following December, dividends to shareholders were suspended, and in an effort to boost sales, a new shirt product called the Dorma brand was introduced. Sales did temporarily improve and the 5% dividend was restored in 1923. But by the end of that year, the board was facing a crisis meeting in December to decide the future, if any, of the company. At the meeting, three

Cutting-room personnel in mid-1930s. Front row includes: Nellie Graham, Joe Callan, Tom McDaid and Willie 'Ginger' Quinn. Back row includes: Charlie Cauley, Davy Knox, Dan McDaid, George Molloy, Jack Anthony and Gordon Wilson.

(Courtesy David Bigger collection)

49

Londonderry Factory Strike – The position of the business was discussed as a result of the Foyle Factory, Londonderry, being closed for the past eight weeks owing to a strike of cutters for an increased rate of pay, causing all the other workers to be shut out for lack of work. Lieut-Col. W.K. Tillie explained the position and reported that negotiations were still going on, and that a further meeting was to be held on 7th August.

The Chairman explained that in these circumstances he was of opinion that the piece goods in stock and contracted for were far in excess of what we could use in a reasonable time. The Meeting concurred with this view, and it was decided that an effort should be made to get some of the contracts cancelled.

Lieut-Col. W.K. Tillie was authorised to arrange this to the best advantage, and if necessary to give a monetary compensation.

Extract from Minute Book relating to the strike of 1920.

options were discussed for survival: to carry on in the hope of trade improvement; amalgamate with some other similar business; or to liquidate. On 15 February 1924, the board of directors proposed liquidation and reconstruction of the company. So, the following month, the Tillie and Henderson (1908) Company was officially liquidated.

The shares of the company were sold to a new syndicate at the greatly reduced value of £83,705, slightly over half of its 1908 value. The largest shareholder of the new board was Colonel Kingsley Tillie – of the third generation of the Tillie family. This new board continued to trade as Tillie and Henderson, and through time the controlling shares eventually passed into the hands of an English family by the name of Fawcett in 1928. They also continued to trade as Tillie and Henderson, though not as a public company with shareholders but as a private one with a board of directors having their registered office in Leigh, Lancaster, England and later relocated in Chester. In the next few years, the shirt industry began to face growing competition, particularly from the so-called English sweatshop manufacturers and the increasing foreign-made shirts, all of which were flooding the market. Radical changes in working practices and production methods were required to meet these challenges if the Derry-made shirt was to become more cost-effective and competitive. As a result, there was a

Extract from Minute Book of 1924 recording the decision to liquidate the company and appoint a liquidator.

Extract from Minute Book showing the value of the company at the time of liquidation.

new emphasis on production methods and factory-floor layout and design, particularly the line system of production.

The line system had been well tried, tested and proved as the most efficient method of production, most notably in America, where Henry Ford was mass producing his Model T Ford motor car. As with the car production process, the shirt began its journey at one end of the line and came off the other end as the finished garment.

In 1935, Tillie and Henderson introduced the conveyor-belt system of production, or 'speed belt' as it was later called; this had transformed the English shirt industry a decade earlier. This new system eliminated the problem of delay inherent in the old system that occurred in the handing out and receiving of bundles of work at the various stages of manufacturing. Each speed belt stretched the length of the machine room, with the girls positioned on each side of the belt. Along the length of the belt there was a permanent divider that in practice meant that each row of girls facing each other made up a separate belt. Each belt or group was numbered and completed its own particular order and was required to complete forty-eight dozen shirts daily.

The cut shirts were brought from the cutting department to the machine rooms by the service women who would then distribute the various component parts to the particular operators. The number of operations on the belt varied with the development and style of the shirt. For example, the slope operation on the belt was originally carried out by the girl who laboriously cut the front part of the shirt to allow for the collar insertion. This operation was eventually transferred to the cutting department, where the design of the front body was altered to allow the band-knife cutter to cut out the collar space in bulk. The sequence of operations would have varied slightly from factory to factory. In Tillies, this sequence was generally as follows: two front stitchers, one for the hem side and one for the buttonside; one buttoner; one girl labelling the yokes; one girl back-fitting and one front-fitting; two banding; two cuff patent-turners; one girl buttonholing; two sleeve piecing; two sleeving; two side seaming; two cuffing; two hemming; the clippers, and finally, the examiners.

Putting this sequence into practice, the shirt began its journey to

The conveyer belts in Tillies circa 1920s. Working on the famous white shirt. (Courtesy David Bigger collection)

53

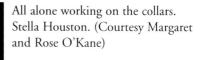

All alone working on the collars. Stella Houston. (Courtesy Margaret and Rose O'Kane)

Three happy collar workers. (L/R): Tessa Gallagher, Margaret Boyle and Frances Brown. (Courtesy Margaret and Rose O'Kane)

Smiling collar workers. Standing (L/R): Emma Bradley, Kathleen Turner and Eileen McKane. Sitting (L/R): Unknown, Josephine Doherty and Unknown. (Courtesy Margaret and Rose O'Kane)

All alone. Frances Browne examines the collars. (Courtesy Margaret and Rose O'Kane)

Collar workers smile for camera. (L/R): Mary O'Donnell, Emma Bradley, Unknown, Margaret Gallagher, Unknown and Unknown. (Courtesy Margaret and Rose O'Kane)

Collar work stops for a photo. Standing (L/R): Lily Gurley, Kathleen McCart (supervisor) and Celine McConomy. Seated: Letta Gormley. (Courtesy Margaret and Rose O'Kane)

completion with the front stitching, the hem side and button side. Next came the buttoner, who put the buttons on the right side front body. After her was the labelling operation, with the operator stitching labels, denoting the size and other details on the yokes that attached the fronts to the back body of the shirt.

This operation was followed by the cuff patent-turners, who basically prepared the cuffs for the stitchers who followed them and completed the cuff. Following on from this was the buttonholer, who machine cut the holes in the front body and the cuffs for the buttons. The sleeve-piece operation came next and involved sewing a small length of material onto the sleeves, which had the effect of taking the tension out of the sleeve to allow elbow movement. Then the sleeves were sewn onto the shirt and the entire shirt was 'closed' by the sideseamer and the cuffs were then attached to the sleeves. The hemmers who followed gave the finished look to the shirt. At the end of the belt was a large table at which all the loose threads were clipped off the garment and they, in turn, passed them on to the examiners who checked for faults. The final examined shirts would be bundled into dozens and put into large trolley baskets and sent by hoist to the laundry to be smoothed, boxed and stocked, awaiting transportation to the then head office in Leigh for retailing.

By the 1930s, retailing had radically changed from the days when William Tillie stockpiled and personally sold his shirts in bulk. Now, with the new era of the high-street department stores, it was they who became the customers and the stores had their own views on materials and design. Soon, Tillies' own brand-name shirts, Sit-rite and Dee Hill, were greatly reduced in bulk as the larger orders from the prestigious Marks and Spencer company dominated production. M&S would eventually become Tillies' major single customer. At the time, this was seen as consolidating employment, which it did for years to come. But in time, this business strategy of having the one major customer became as much a vulnerable situation for the supplier as it was an advantage.

As the major customer offering substantial contracts, M&S was in a strong position to influence changes in working practices and production techniques within the factory. An initial change to working

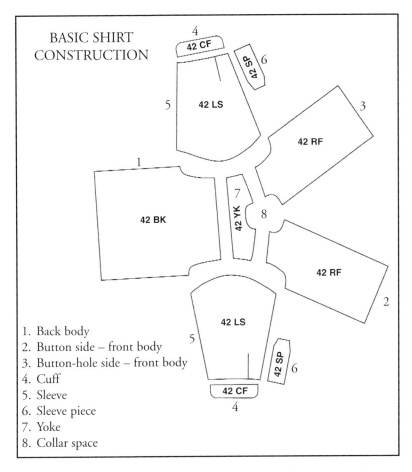

BASIC SHIRT CONSTRUCTION

4
42 CF
42 SP
6
5   42 LS
3
42 RF
1
7
42 YK
8
42 BK
42 RF
2
42 LS
5
42 SP
6
42 CF
4

1. Back body
2. Button side – front body
3. Button-hole side – front body
4. Cuff
5. Sleeve
6. Sleeve piece
7. Yoke
8. Collar space

practices involved replacing the usual method of despatching shirts ie, in a large container to a central depot in Leigh, Lancaster, for customer distribution. The new method involved the shirts being despatched from the Derry factory direct to individual M&S stores all over Great Britain. So lengthy was the new procedure that four extra men were employed to assist the two regular shirt packers, Dan Doran and Sam Bierney. And during the holiday rush periods, when the volume of shirts to be despatched was heavy, some male cutters were required to work overtime to meet the demand. Also, because of the large ground space required to hold all the large cartons packed with shirts awaiting M&S to 'draw off', as and when required, the stockroom had to be relocated. All the cloth stock that had been previously housed in the despatch area now had to be relocated to the top floor of the factory, which was five storeys high.

For this to be done, a permanent large iron conveyor-type belt had to be erected in the factory yard. This was a rather frail construction and great care had to be taken when placing the cloth parcels on it so as not to overload it. This frequently happened because there were several men at the bottom, loading, and only two regular stockroom men, Ronnie Young and Jack Allen, at the top, unloading. Not surprisingly, a few parcels would come hurtling down as those men at the bottom scattered and swore. The cloth stock relocation had a knock-on effect, and the cutting department had also to be switched from the third floor to the top floor to be convenient to the cloth supply. The machine rooms also had to be relocated at one time.

A further requirement of Marks and Spencer resulted from market-research surveys carried out by them all over their Great Britain stores and was to radically transform cutting-room production techniques. M&S established how many of the different sizes of shirts were selling in relation to each other. This enabled them to establish a ratio of sizes that accompanied each of their orders. For example:

Sizes:	14	14½	15	15½	16	16½	17	17½	18
Shirts:	1	1	3	8	6	4	2	2	1

Applying this ratio to an order for 10,000 dozen shirts presented something of a mathematical problem for the particular cutter planning the lay. The lay-planning task became even more difficult when cloth utilisation had to be taken into account. So, the 'scrambled' lay was introduced. This involved all the different sizes and all the different component parts of the shirt being intermingled with each other. Since there was a particular yardage of material per shirt length, this made the task of the lay planner even more difficult and akin to solving a jigsaw puzzle. It was equally difficult for the band-

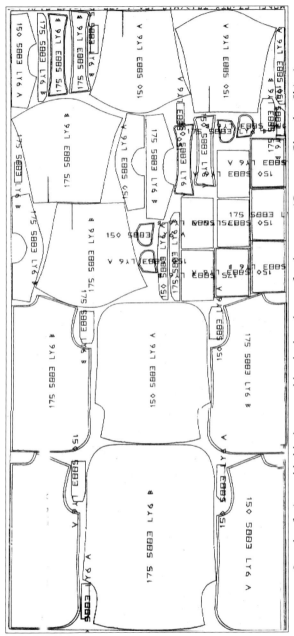

Sample of a 'scrambled lay' prepared by the lay planner for the cutter. (Courtesy Glenaden Shirts)

59

knife cutter, who had to customise the lay to allow for the chances of cutting a wrong size.

With M&S involvement came an exceptionally high standard of quality control, particularly in the shirt measurements that were critical almost to a sixteenth of an inch. To this end, a quality manager, Brian Nolan, was appointed by Tillies. They were also interested in the quality and ability of future employees. At their insistence, Tillies appointed a personnel officer who was interviewed for the job by a Marks and Spencer representative.

Occasionally, M&S top managers would come over to the Derry factory for a walkabout inspection. Advance word of such a visit increased anxiety levels among local department managers and supervisors and expectancy among the cutters who got weekend overtime cleaning the entire factory. Machinists had to clean down their workplaces and all work had to be covered (and sometimes hidden away from view), as everything except the rats was washed, polished and shined.

On a more regular basis, M&S quality-control representatives made visits to the Derry factory to carry out random inspection checks on the shirts. They would go into the despatch and select a number of boxed shirts, open and examine them for quality – and particularly measurements. It was said that prior to these visits, Cissie Kelly, the laundry manageress, would secretly sprinkle Holy Water on the cartons of shirts in the belief that Divine Intervention would repair any overlooked faults, such was the dread of orders being rejected.

Indeed on one occasion, M&S did reject a small order of 300 white shirts which were subsequently purchased by a local entrepreneur. On another occasion, all Tillies' supervisors, together with Brian Nolan, were brought over to Manchester on a quality-control exercise, as supervisor Stella McDaid recalls:

When we landed in Manchester we were taken into one of their stores and each supervisor picked a dozen shirts at random and took them up to the boardroom. Every one of us had to open up the shirts and go through them with a notepad and pencil and write down all the faults we found. Then someone came behind us and re-examined and found faults. I'll never forget it.

In between these visits from M&S, George Fawcett, the managing director of Tillies, would often visit. He was a rather small, neatly dressed man with a handkerchief protruding out of the top pocket who always appeared to be walking on his toes. His arrival would keep everyone on *their* toes and created anxiety for the local management who would have been aware of the results and recommendations of the most recent M&S visits. Some of these recommendations or complaints would inevitably take Fawcett to the cutting room, where the staff were always expecting him. Sammy Moore, the cutting-room manager, had the room forewarned: "Watch yourself. Wee George is coming." This meant, *Don't be standing around like a tourist when Fawcett is here.*

Fawcett's visit was more of a nuisance value than anything else. He was always wanting a quarter of an inch off here and something added there, though he did appear to know what he was talking about. Certainly the women spoke highly of his ability. Here's one woman's memory:

> Wee Fawcett could do every part of the shirt except the hemming. He could have sat down and done the cuffing, the fitting, the banding – you name it, he could do it. One girl had trouble with the sleeve piecing, and he told her she was taking too much into the guide and he sat down and showed her what to do.

By the autumn of 1950, the shirt industry in the city went into a deep recession, the worst since the late 1920s. By October 1951, it was reported that 1,000 Derry shirt workers had been paid off. Those still working were on a shorter working week, which in Tillies meant working four days one week and two days the following week. But short time was not a success and Tillies paid off 300 workers, which brought the unemployed shirt workers total in the city to slightly over 2,000.

There was some controversy that the total included a high number of workers from across the border who, at that time, required a permit to work in Northern Ireland, but the Minister of Commerce rejected this. He commented that: "Under the Safeguard of Employment Act

1947, no cancellation of work permit had been made but that 167 were not renewed," which could be described as a more subtle method of cancellation.

With no immediate signs of a recovery in the trade, there was general regret within the city's Shirt Manufacturing Federation that they did not tender for government army-shirt contracts, which had gone mostly to Italian manufacturers. Government contracts were certainly worth winning, particularly since rearmament and recruitment were in full swing after the war and two million army shirts were available for tendering. To this end, Stephen McGonagle of the Union of Tailor and Garment Workers suggested a strategy of co-operation during a meeting with the Shirt Manufacturing Federation. The strategy, that all the factories should agree not to be in competition with each other and that their costing should have little if any variation, was agreed. The Derry factories submitted their tenders.

Out of all the factories that submitted, only six had received telegrams by the end of December, confirming that they had been successful. Immediately, the unions claimed there was discrimination in favour of the Belfast manufacturers. Stephen McGonagle protested to the British Ministry of Supply that: "Orders for only between one-eighth and one-sixth of the two million shirts have come to Derry." He estimated that that was only five or six weeks' work.

Trade unions had made their appearance in Tillies during the 1930s and had become more active in the late 1940s, when they were stronger, with the girls being more militant, and negotiation was the vehicle of compromise. The unions successfully achieved holiday pay for the workers, who previously received no pay for the two weeks in August when the factory was closed. This breakthrough was followed later, in 1956, when Tillies was reputed to be the first factory in Great Britain to introduce the guaranteed day's payment. In practice, this meant that the girls would now be paid should they have to sit idle waiting for work to come to them where previously they could have been sent home.

Unfortunately, and despite the government contracts, short-time working and pay-offs were to become a recurring feature of the employment pattern within the Derry shirt industry as foreign imports began to increase. The answer to foreign imports, which were also affecting British industry in general, was thought to be more modernisation and automation. As a safeguard, the government introduced the Redundancy Act in the early 1960s to financially help the expected widespread redundant workforce as automation further developed. In the 1960s, a feeble attempt at automation had been made in Tillies' cutting room with the introduction of the electric-driven cart for spreading the material on the tables. In appearance, it was a solid-metal frame construction, having two roller bars, one on top of the other, through which the material was fed, taking the tension off it.

Coping with cloth tension was extremely difficult, especially after the introduction of man-made fibres, particularly nylon with its inherent stretching properties. These roller bars on the cart had a small wheel attachment that the operator worked to adjust the movement of the rollers and keep the material falling straight on the table. Also, there was a cable along the entire length of the table that the operator pulled on to start or stop the cart, though at times this was not very reliable. At either end of the table there was a little wooden block that automatically stopped the cart as the two small wheels on the undercarriage of the cart made contact. This particular system was also not very reliable. The end of the table was only about the length of the cart away from the window on the top floor, so the operator was frequently seen and heard screaming and running after the cart to have it stopped before it crash-landed out on Carlisle Square.

In time, the electric cart was followed by the introduction of the automatic-press cutting machine that could cut out the smaller components of the shirt, collar, cuff, and yokes simultaneously. In practice, the cutter would put the block of material on the large moveable tray attached to the machine and place the steel shapes of the various parts on the material.

Next, he would push the tray into the machine to coincide with the falling and lifting of the pressure area. When doing this, if the shape happened to topple over, or he mistimed his action, there was not much left of the shape. Although the machine saved cutting time, it was not an economical use of material, because extra space was required between the shapes to allow for the movement of the cloth under the pressure. In the end, the machine was primarily used to cut the firmer collar and cuff linings.

These two pieces of machinery were followed by the multiple lay-maker, which basically duplicated the master lays previously pencilled by the cutter, and of the three it was the most successful.

If Tillies, and indeed the entire shirt industry in Derry, were to survive and become more efficient, economical, and enterprising, then automation was only a beginning. Attention was now focusing on a new method of production to replace the conveyor belts, which were now seen to be antiquated and a totally inefficient method of production that had outlived its time. By the 1960s, a new production method soon became the buzz phrase within the Derry shirt trade – Time Study Engineering (TSE). TSE was introduced into Tillies in 1965. In theory, work engineering was to significantly increase production and reduce cost. In practice, it was to radically change working relationships, practices and conditions within the factories.

The Derry factory girl was soon to discover that the clock moved much faster than the speed belt, and the working day was now to be measured in minutes rather than hours. Undoubtedly, from the management's perspective, TSE was a more subtle, sophisticated and scientific approach to assessing and achieving the individual production potential of the worker.

From the girl's perspective, the idea of her wages and earning power depending on individual ability was both a frightening and apprehensive situation in comparison to the speed belt system, where each girl did a fixed amount for a fixed wage. Now, with work study, earnings were under the individual's own control. The faster the girl worked, the more she earned; the slower she worked, the less she earned. Time study introduced an entirely new concept of shirt production. It also, however, became a highly contentious and controversial issue, not only in Tillies, but also in other factories.

The story of Tillie and Henderson, however, is not just about the factory's technological advances and production methods or the history of various shirt-making processes. It is about the mothers, daughters, grannies and aunts (not forgetting the minority of male employees) who worked over many decades in Tillies and they have contributed in the following chapters their memories, images and anecdotes to bring the real story to life.

The historic Tillie and Henderson factory in all its glory in late 1960s. (Courtesy Brian Nolan and Patrick Hegarty)

65

The Factory Horn

The factory horn was a familiar sound in Derry during the twentieth century. Groups of young girls and women in their traditional formation of arms linked together would converge on the shirt factories. The working day in Tillies was organised from 8.00am to 12.45pm and 2.00pm to 6.00pm, though this, like everything else in Tillies, was to change through time. There were two soundings of the morning horn: the first at 7.50am and the second blast on the hour. It was the same in the afternoon: the first sounding at 1.50pm and the second on the hour. The person responsible for sounding the horn was Paddy Morrison, the boiler man, who started at six o'clock in the morning to get the boiler at full steam or there would have been no sound from the horn.

Sadie Morris, who was a smoother in Tillies for over twenty years, remembers going to work from Creggan in the 1950s:

> Five or six of us would meet at the roundabout at the top of Westway every morning, link arms and walk down Bligh's Lane, talking about the 'bars' (the boys), up through the Bogside or sometimes the Dark Lane and down the Abercorn Road.

From Creggan to Tillies. (L/R): Angela and Eithne Duffy set out for their work. (Courtesy Eithne Glackin)

66

Their linked arms were quickly separated when the horn finished and they had to dash up the iron steps of Tillies or across the wooden gangway to the alternative entrance before the doors were closed.

Standing at the top of the iron steps, with his hand on the door bars waiting to pull them shut immediately the horn stopped sounding, was the familiar (if not too popular) figure of Dan Doran, who was the factory caretaker and packer. After the horn stopped, and as soon as a gap appeared between the girls coming up the steps, Dan closed the doors and then had to endure the wrath of the girls' tongues as they complained bitterly about being locked out. Interestingly, some one of the doors was always that little bit slower in closing, particularly when one of the department managers was there. Sometimes it was the entrance at the top of the steps and sometimes the door at the end of the gangway. Undoubtedly, this was a shrewd management ploy, for it would not have helped production if large numbers had been locked out every day.

Brian Nolan, the last factory manager of Tillies, when asked what production problem caused him the most trouble, confirmed this: "Attendance would have been a priority. If one section was hit by

Latecomers' route into the factory. (Courtesy Peter McCarron)

Tillies' strongest worker, Dick the pet horse, with Tom Hannigan. (Courtesy Brian Nolan and Patrick Hegarty)

absenteeism, you were in serious bother, particularly if it was a key section like the front stitching." This was because front stitching was the first operation on the conveyor belt as the shirt started its journey to completion; without the front stitcher, production was seriously threatened.

Those workers who were locked out would race frantically down Tillie's Brae to the Foyle Road entrance in the hope that the hall or office doors were open and that Davy Neely, who was assistant factory manager to John Reed in the early 1950s, was not lurking about. Should these entrances be locked, a last hope was to run up the factory yard (if the large iron gates were open), pass the horse stable and go through the wash house or boiler house areas and up the back stairs into the machine rooms. The yard gates were generally open a few mornings in the week, depending on whether Tom Hannigan, the carter, had to harness his pet horse, Dick, and take a consignment of shirts down to the Quay or collect a shipment of cloth from the docks to bring back. Indeed, Dick never lifted a hoof to move anywhere until he got his daily gravy ring from Cissie Kelly, the laundry manageress, who spoiled him rotten.

Through the yard was a favourite route of the Madden sisters, Kathleen and Phyllis, who lived practically next door to the factory on Foyle Road, though they were still not the best of timekeepers. They never had any problem with the route until one morning, when slipping into their machine room late, they confronted Davy Neely sitting on the bench. As they hurried passed, the voice rang out: "Kathleen, one moment please." Kathleen froze on the spot as Davy approached and handed her a small brown parcel. Everyone had guessed what it was. It only required Kathleen to open it, which she did, half-smiling, to reveal an alarm clock, and any thoughts she may have had that it was a gift were quickly dispelled: "You can pay something every week to Miss McKelvey in the office for it, and don't forget to set the bloody alarm."

Phyllis Madden was heard to utter a few choice phrases of her own as she made her way down the room. It was said of the Madden girls that because they lived so close to the factory and had so much time for their lunch, that if they took a 'wee sleep' they would inevitably oversleep, and the morning panic was repeated when the two o'clock horn blew. Habitual latecomers would generally have been dismissed, but Davy knew his workforce and knew the Madden sisters were exceptional workers who could easily make up any lost production.

Davy Neely, or Big Davy as he was called by the girls, was a tall, large-framed man with a mainly expressionless face, which some called his 'factory face', and he always had witty remarks. To some, he was seen as stern and unapproachable, while others had no such impressions and would approach him with complaints and suggestions like: "Mr Neely, why don't you run a factory dance sometime?"

"Listen, dear," Davy would reply. "I've enough clowns in here to run a circus."

The Maddens were not the only ones to receive 'Davy's clocks', the most notable other person being Joan Kennedy, who was also something of a personality. Because she also lived practically next door to Tillies, Joan often boasted to her co-workers that she could go from the bed to work in ten minutes, but this was more fiction than truth. On one of the many occasions that Joan was locked out, she devised a unique and humorous plan of how to get into her work, as one of her co-workers, Berna McShane, a hemmer, recalls:

> Dan Doran locked her out, so Joan went into the children's play park beside the factory and started sliding down the banana slide and waving to all the girls in the factory who were looking out at her. So Davy sent a girl out for her to bring her in, for there was no work being done.

She was equally the centre of attraction at times inside the factory, as when she was often seen washing her hair at the jaw box (a large delft sink) outside the women's toilet in preparation for the weekend dances. If any worker stood out amongst all the 800-plus women who worked in Tillies at the time, it was Joan Kennedy. She looked as if she had stepped straight out of the musical *West Side Story*, with her distinctive short blonde hair, blue denim skirt, white bobby socks and

Joan Kennedy, one of the best-known personalities in Tillies.
(Courtesy Ronnie Kennedy)

plimsolls. The musical could be said to have been almost re-enacted on a Friday night in the Embassy Ballroom, when Joan was the centre of attraction, jitterbugging and jiving with American personnel from the Waterside Naval Communications Base.

For those girls who could not manage to get into the factory, most returned home to face the music of a possible lecture from their mothers on the loss of a half-day's wages. Some, however, preferred to hang around in the hope that one of the department managers would come down to the Foyle Road entrance to see if there were any key workers still there. The laundry supervisor, Cissie Kelly, regularly came down and justified this latecomers' concession by maintaining:

"They must be very anxious to work if they are still hanging about."
Some other supervisors were more determined to get their key workers into their work, according to Roisin Gallagher (née McAllister):

> Vera McConnell would send me out to Kitty Clifford's house who
> lived next door to Tillies on the Foyle Road and told me to knock
> hard till I got an answer and tell her to come into her work. I was
> also sent up to other houses in Howard Street and sometimes the
> girl would come in and others would be sick or something.

The morning drama was always repeated again in the afternoon,
and one latecomer, Suzy McCourt, also had a very original plan to get
into her work. Suzy was something of a make-up artist and would put
talcum power on her face to pretend to be sick if she wanted out early
or as an excuse for being late. The talc gave her a ghostly appearance
similar to the London Gothic craze of the 1960s; and it worked nine
times out of ten. The tenth time involved Suzy being confronted by
her then department manager, Brian Nolan, who was later to become
factory manager. She told him a very imaginative story:

> "What happened you?"
> "Aw dear, Mr Nolan, don't start me the day. I was coming down
> Abercorn Road when an Alsatian bounced at me and pinned me
> behind a woman's door and I couldn't get out."
> "No, not the day, Suzy, you have too much powder on that
> face."
> "I beg your pardon, Mr Nolan; I'm pure white with fear."
> "Not at all, Suzy."
> "Wait till I tell you this, Mr Nolan, even a rose must fade."

Humour can work sometimes when excuses fail, and the manager
found it difficult to send Suzy home; besides, he was also aware that
she was an excellent worker.

Buns, Banter and the 'Bars'

Once inside with their coats hung up, the girls took their positions on the speed belt, but not before the 'rat check'. Around the machines were picnic areas for the rats, since there was no canteen and the girls would eat at their machines and spill crumbs all over the place. Monday mornings were particularly apprehensive for the girls, as the rats had had the freedom of the factory over the weekend.

The girls would start kicking their work boxes and rattling their scissors on the machine top to flush the rats out, but some rats were more adventurous than others, as Kathleen Duffy, a patent-turner, recalls: "Annie Doherty came in one Monday morning and reached for the drawer, pulled it out and a rat jumped out. She nearly brought the place around her with panic."

When the cry "Rats!" was heard, some girls would stand up on their stools to be safe and on one occasion Celine Clark, a hemmer, thought she would be safer standing on the conveyer belt (which was not switched on at the time) only to see a rat running down the belt towards her. Both jumped off the belt at the same time.

No place appeared to be out of bounds for the rats, as one of the mechanics, Seamus McLaughlin, discovered when he put on his coat and a rat came scurrying out of the sleeve after apparently having a chew to itself. Seamus never wore that coat again.

Rats were not exclusive to Tillies. All the large shirt factories would have had their rat population, because the cloth and the paper wrapping were on the rats' menu.

The replacement of the wooden floors with tarmacadam helped in reducing the rat population in Tillies, but the biggest single factor was Dan Doran's rat cages, which he set before locking up the factory at night. Dan knew all the rats' highways and byways and placed his traps accordingly, and in the morning he could be seen walking through the machine rooms, proudly carrying the trapped rats on his way to the ash pit. When he came back through the machine room, some of the girls would sing the parody: "There was a rat, a rat as big as a bloody cat, in Dan Doran's cage."

With the rat check completed and the conveyor belt switched on, the shirt began its journey to completion from one end to the other, and in between lay all the trials, troubles, and tribulation of the girls' working day.

On the speed belt, there were two girls for most operations. They would alternatively lift off the shirt that was placed on a line drawn on the belt as it came towards them. If any girl was not ready for the next shirt, she would lift it off and keep it to do at a later time, or she would let it pass and her unfinished work would be brought back to her. Those girls who fell behind would have to work overtime at their own expense to get cleared for the next day.

Individual girls had their own solution to the problem of falling behind, as was the case with Eithne Duffy, a sideseamer: "I remember being piled up one day and I ran home for my dinner and ran back again to be in half an hour before the time to get the work done."

Another girl had a more effective and immediate method of playing catch-up. Kathleen Duffy recalls:

Bridie Nash used to get behind and there would be a big pile of shirts beside her. Bridie was able to stop the belt somehow with her foot and then a mechanic was sent for to fix the problem.

A more devious practice of playing catch-up among some girls was the mysterious disappearance of the shuttle from the machine (this was the container of thread underneath the machine and known as the 'underthread'). This effectively immobilised the machine, which meant in practice that the worker coming after the girl whose shuttle was mysteriously lost could have the time it took to find the shuttle to play catch-up. The shuttle was inevitably found on the floor, further down the belt where it rolled after it allegedly fell off the machine.

Each speed belt, which was numbered, finished a complete order, and before the introduction of bonus systems in the early 1960s, the girls were paid according to the specified amounts they had to do. For example, at one time an individual hemmer had to do twenty-four dozen shirts per day to earn her wages. The method of payment was very basic. There were no cheques or payment through banks; it was much more direct, as Stella McDaid, a cuff stitcher, recalls:

> Davy Neely came into the room carrying a big tray full of small cups, like big eggcups, with the money in them; Miss McKelvey from the office was with him. The girls would all leave their machines and march single file up to Miss McKelvey who would call out your number to Davy and he would empty the cup into your hand. If there were any notes – if you would be so lucky – he would lay them out flat on your hand with the coins in the middle.

The speed belt was stopped to allow for a ten-minute tea break in the mornings and afternoons. At that particular time in the early 1950s, there was no canteen in the factory, so everyone had to make their own arrangements for tea. Stella McDaid recalls:

> You had a wee poke of tea and you went down to the boiler room with tea pots, snuff tins with wire handles on them, you name it, and lined them all up on the floor for the hot water and you had to be on the ball if you didn't want to wait all morning. For some girls would come along and move their pots to the top of the line; on the way upstairs again, you got scalded.

Tea making in the cutting room was more orthodox, with the availability of a gas ring and a large tea pot. Nora Bradley usually made it and collected fivepence (2p) each week towards expenses.

The tea was always ready and waiting well before the break, as were the buns that were ordered from Tracey's shop adjacent to the factory in John Street. Young 'clippies' (or message girls as they were more commonly called) were allowed out with their bundles of notes for orders. Since all the orders were on credit, all notes had to be authenticated by the signature of the guarantor, as one former clippie explains: "You wrote on the note what you required and your name had to go on it. Then you took it up to Nora Bradley in the cutting room who signed and stamped it."

The orders were not all for buns. Some were also for sweets and chips, should the girls be working overtime. There was a time when nobody was allowed out. It was probably due to the ingenuity of the girls to get bags of chips when they were working overtime that lifted the ban. Bridget Doherty started working in Tillies in 1935 and remembers a particular incident of how the chips were smuggled into the factory:

> We would throw strings out the window on the Foyle Road end of the factory and the girl would tie the parcel of chips from Tracey's for us to pull up. Then one day Davy Neely was looking out the window and saw this parcel rising up past the window, and it didn't take him long to solve the mystery. But he was more amused than annoyed.

Generally speaking, at that time there was a good working relationship throughout the factory between management and workers, to the extent that the girls agreed to work until 7.00pm during the week of their annual religious retreat week. This was to facilitate the completion of a hurried order for Marks and Spencer. The management acknowledged the girls' effort with a personal message in their pay from George Fawcett, the Works Director in the Chester headquarters, expressing the firm's thanks.

The two cutting-room cleaners, Ginny McLaughlin and Minnie Caldwell, always went to Tracey's for the cutting-room workers, and it was said of Minnie that she always gave the personal touch when ordering the buns in Tracey's. She would call out: "Two cookies for Jimmy Doherty, a bap with butter on for Eileen Lynch, a gravy ring for Mickey Browne," and on it went. Some of the girls preferred to bring bread and have it toasted by the smoothing irons used by the patent-turners (collar and neckband smoothers). That gave it a special taste. One particular patent-turner, Lily McSherry, a big, well-built, strong woman, put her whole weight on the iron when toasting, with the result that the toast was wafer-thin, roasting hot, very tasty, brittle and definitely dangerous for those with loose or false

Thank-you note from Works Director George Fawcett.
(Courtesy Michael Lynch)

teeth. Some girls, in the interest of hygiene, preferred their bread toasted without taking it out of the bag; either way, the toast had a special flavour similar to the modern toasties.

In contrast to the outside trade with Tracey's, Tillies had its own indoor market where anything and everything could be bought on tick (credit) until Friday. In the machine rooms, home-made apple tarts could be bought from the likes of Maisie McLaughlin, Maggie McIntyre, Aggie Brennan, Ginny Duddy and others, who brought them into the factory in baskets, tin boxes and paper bags. The cheaper cigarettes smuggled across the border were plentiful, while sweets, biscuits and chocolate were sold by Charlie Cauley in the cutting room. He brought these in from his outside shop. He was also something of an interest-free money lender to some of the apprentice cutters who always were stuck for a few bob and would get a loan from him on a Monday and pay him back on Friday. This would be repeated on a weekly basis to the confusion of Charlie who didn't know who owed what for how long. Charlie operated a part-time shop from his band-knife machine and had the monopoly on the religious and fancy goods. During the annual religious retreats for women, his band-knife machine took on the appearance of a Holy Shop, with rosaries, crucifixes and prayer books displayed. He was able to do this because his machine was strategically placed and he could easily see Davy Neely before Davy could see him, should he be on a walkabout.

Women from different religious and political backgrounds worked together in all the city factories, though some factories would have a majority from a Unionist background, others a majority from a Nationalist background. Tillie and Henderson's reputation as a majority Nationalist factory was established as far back as 1883, when the workers were involved in a dispute of a sectarian nature. At that time, the then Lord Mayor of Dublin, Charles Dawson MP, intended to avail of the city's Guildhall to speak on franchise reform. Permission to use the hall was refused and the medical officer of Tillie and Henderson, Sir William Millar MD JP, was alleged to have been one of the main objectors. As a portion of Millar's wage resulted from deductions from the workers' wages, there were calls for him to be replaced by a Catholic doctor. Millar and the Protestant workers in the factory were subjected to jeering by the Catholic workforce to such an extent that the steam was turned off as department managers unsuccessfully attempted to control and calm the situation.

The incident escalated during the lunch break when the police, some on horseback, baton-charged a group of Tillies' workers outside the factory. Though some of the girls were jostled and their clothes torn, little serious injury other than bruising occurred. Tension further increased at night as the workers held a rally that resulted in stone throwing at the police. The disturbances closed the factory for three days and though no workers were dismissed, the loss of three days' pay would have been punishment enough – and the fact that Millar remained the factory medical officer. The incident clearly identified Tillie and Henderson as having a predominantly Catholic workforce, and as such, the girls and the building, which was situated at the bottom of the predominantly Protestant Fountain area, became annual targets of rogue elements during the August Protestant celebrations at the close of the nineteenth century.

Such serious and disruptive confrontations did not appear to have spilled over into the twentieth century. Apart from some harmless banter, the girls worked harmoniously together. On one occasion, a particular girl, known to be a supporter of the Orange Order, was persuaded that she was required at the top of the collar room, and when she left her machine, the Nationalist girls removed her stool. Returning, she had to stand, which was the plan of the deception, whereupon the guilty girls began singing the Soldiers' Song, with Kathleen Hone, a collar worker, leading the banter: "There now, Sandra, didn't we say that one day you would stand for our National Anthem."

Sandra was quick with her reply: "Is that what they call that tune?"

Glasses off for a photo. Collar worker Kathleen Hone.
(Courtesy Margaret and Rose O'Kane)

In the laundry department, it was said that one Maggie Fleming would come in wearing her Orange Lily on the Twelfth and take a bit of banter from some of the girls. But she had her own back when those same girls would come to their work on St Patrick's Day wearing shamrocks, about which Maggie made the inquiry: "What's that auld weed?"

The laundry department, like the other rooms, was free from serious sectarianism. As one smoother, Sadie Morris, put it: "Everyone got on all right. We sang most of the day; visitors liked to hear the workers singing."

Other 'bits of fun' almost resulted in dismissals, as when an Orange Order parade marching across the bridge towards Tillies was greeted with a Tricolour hanging from a window. A delegation from the march lodged a complaint in the general office and an investigation later into the incident discovered that the offending Tricolour was a combination of three coloured scarves that nobody apparently owned.

On another occasion, it had been rumoured that a particular male employee of Tillies had been seen removing a Nationalist election poster supporting a Dr Cavanagh. Within the factory, the particular man received a message that he was required in Number Two machine room and on entering was immediately pelted with thread bobbins. Reacting to the incident, Davy Neely, the factory manager at the time, randomly selected and took four workers to the top of the room and told them they were being dismissed. One of the four was Kitty McSherry, who wasn't easily threatened: "Look down that room, Mr Neely, everybody is watching. If you put us out, they're coming out along with us."

Whether the threat was real or not, confrontation was avoided. Davy replied, with slightly raised voice: "Get quickly down that room; I don't want to see youse again."

The degree of tolerance and non-sectarianism among the girls was highlighted one Twelfth of August by Maisie McLaughlin:

> Dorothy Alford asked Brian Nolan, her department manager, to let her out to see the Orange parade and he had no objections so long as her work was cleared up. But Dorothy was never cleared up, so Lily Brown and me helped to clear up her work and she got out to the Orange march.

In the cutting room on the Twelfth, the Orange parade across the bridge was always watched with interest and a fair share of banter by the mixed workforce. They would watch Jack Allen, who worked in the cloth store adjacent to the cutting room, marching with his black suit, white gloves, hard hat and sword at the head of the parade. Willie 'Ginger' Quinn, a staunch Nationalist, would match banter with Unionists Jim Crawford and big Jack Anthony, and it generally lasted for the better part of the day, with Davy Neely doing a little harmless 'stirring it up'. Jack Allen was later to become involved in local politics and became the first of two Tillies' workers to become Mayor of the city, the other being the SDLP's Hugh Doherty, a painter in the factory.

The strategic value of Tillies (in having a panoramic view of Craigavon Bridge) was quickly recognised by the British army as an observation post to monitor the Civil Rights marches. Approached about this by the army authorities at the beginning of 1970, factory manager Brian Nolan was reluctant to concede to the army's request on the argument that it could result in a degree of disruption. Passing the request on to his superiors in Chester, Brian was told that it was probably the case that the army could use emergency powers and that it would be difficult to prevent them from using the building anyway. Eventually, two squaddies from the Queen's Regiment occupied the small attic room, accessed from the cutting room on the top floor of the factory, and were billeted there on camp beds. Remarkably few, if any, of the workers were aware of their presence, so covert was the operation, though a few of the cutting staff caught a random glimpse of a soldier coming from an early morning wash in one of the unused toilets in the adjacent and vacated C department.

Apart from the morning and afternoon tea breaks, there was also a five-minute break every hour when the speed belt was stopped and those who smoked went into the 'parlour' (euphemism for toilet). It was appropriately named, for that was the room in Derry homes where visitors were taken and everyone sat around and chatted. This was precisely what the girls did except they had to stand smoking and chatting, and the décor was far from relaxing. As one supervisor remarked:

It was dark and dismal, like the dark hole of Calcutta. There was no washing facility except for a big large, deep delft sink, or jaw box, as some called it, with the one cold water tap resting on a very flimsy looking bracket immediately outside the toilet.

The chat generally involved around the 'bars' ie, who was going with whom, though talk about local fellas faded whenever the navy was in town. Some of the girls liked to date a sailor and then talk about it in the parlour to a hushed audience. Phyllis McCourt (née Moran) remembers the parlour scene:

> You always went into the parlour at the break and you always went in to hear the bars. For the British navy and all were on the go then, you know, and you heard all the bars about the girls going out with the navy men the night before, and of course someone would say: "Here, take a smoke, Phyllis," and you just tried it to be one of the gang, and that was you caught then. And the best of it was you couldn't afford to smoke, for you hadn't the money.

With smoking a popular and expensive habit among the girls, 'passing the butt' was a popular ritual in all the different toilets, as was the talk about sailors. Sadie Morris recalls her trips into the laundry parlour:

> You just couldn't afford to buy fags, so the butt was passed between four of us at a time, and if you were the last, you got your lips singed sucking it and there was always the chat about the sailors. When the ships were in, some sailors would be waiting outside the factory for the girl they had met the last time they were in and the girl would have a head full of curlers ready for the 'date' that night and when she saw him she wouldn't come down the steps but would go out the Abercorn door so he wouldn't see her.

Even if the fleet wasn't in, there was a permanent supply of Americans from the American Naval Communications Base in the Waterside, and it was talk about them that attracted the most interest in the parlour, as Mary Lynch, a front stitcher, remembers:

One time in the parlour, the talk was about the Americans from the base and one girl let it slip that one of them who she knew wanted to meet a red-haired factory girl with freckles at Littlewoods corner on that next Friday night. About four of us went that night to Littlewoods corner, me with my leg tan and high heels and, sure enough, he turned up and, true to his word again, he was attracted to a lovely red-haired girl called Margaret Barr. It was all only a bit of fun on all our part and nothing serious came out of it.

It would be no exaggeration to say that some girls in Tillies and other factories knew as much about the comings and goings of ships as the naval authorities did. This was particularly so whenever Peggy Brady, another personality in Tillies, could be heard shouting as she humped large bundles of work into the machine rooms: "The *Reliant* and the *Redoubtable* are coming in at the weekend, girls." She must have overheard some girls chatting, for Peggy herself declared no interest in the sailors and held strong views about marriage in general, which she aired frequently: "No back room, a bundle of sticks, five Woodbine and a greyhound for me. It's a semidetached with a fitted kitchen and stainless steel sink."

Peggy had a very physical job. Together with Florrie Logue, Olive Fleming and Mary McAllister, she carried large bundles of the cut shirts from the cutting room to the machine rooms. She would also carry the large rolls of cloth on her shoulder from the hoist to the cutting table, where it was shaded, before being spread on the table. This was to ensure that the finished shirt wouldn't have different shades.

The male cutters had no specified five minutes in every hour but tended to go for a smoke whenever their nicotine levels fell. The men's parlour, like the women's, was a small, dark and dismal place, and a definite health hazard. When there were a number of men in smoking, it was like a gas chamber. And the smell was far from fresh. One particular cutter, Jim Crawford, contributed most to the fog, for he would chain-smoke between three and four of the more expensive Gallaher Blues cigarettes on each visit and would stamp out large butts to the envy of the apprentice cutters who had to nick their cheaper Wild Woodbine (which they'd got on tick). Because of its interior construction – a wooden beam connecting both opposite walls – the apprentices would use the beam as a tennis net. With one player standing on each side, they would hand-hit a paper ball over it to score the points.

Directly above the beam was a wooden water gully which carried a water overflow. At times, the paper balls would land in the gully, where they would remain, and the players would simply make a new ball and continue. Through time, water started to run down the walls of the parlour and the factory chief engineer, Eddie Farren, was consulted about the problem, which he concluded, to the amusement of the cutters, was the result of condensation. However, as time revealed, the engineer was well aware of the cause of the problem and that some sackings could result if he gave his more accurate assessment. The tennis tournaments immediately stopped and relocated to the ground-floor despatch area.

The despatch area was but one of what could be called 'women-free zones', which were safe refuges for mechanics, cutters and the occasional department manager escaping women pressure. During the 1950s and '60s, there were approximately thirty-three men, five apprentices and upwards of 800 women and young girls employed in Tillies. The other zones were the carpenters' and painters' workshop, the boiler house and the stockroom. Hospitality was always assured in the boiler room, with its constant supply of hot water for making a cup of tea or a wash and shave if one was late getting into work. The carpenters' shop resembled a conference centre at times, with cutters, mechanics, carpenters and painters all debating and discussing world and local affairs.

In the carpenters' shop, Joe McCourt, Mickey McLaughlin and Joe O'Reilly could always be relied upon to make a few 'rickety wheels' for the Derry City football matches; Hugh Doherty and Barney Quigg were always available to paint them red and white. One of the work-study engineers, John Barber, managed to make himself a guitar in the carpenters' shop in his spare time, though not many said they heard it play. The carpenters' shop was always clean and tidy thanks to the constant brushing up by the young cleaner whose enthusiasm had to be restrained by Joe McCourt: "Son, if you keep on cleaning away the sawdust when I am working, the bosses will think there is no work being done down here at all."

The despatch area became something of a social club during the lunch break, with activities including darts matches, general knowledge contests, paper football games and card schools. Card schools were the most popular until the discovery of one such school during working hours resulted in suspensions. Having operated within a well-hidden area behind a wall of strategically placed cardboard shirt cartons, one particular game got slightly out of hand, with someone shouting: "C'mon, put your money up or pack it in." The commotion was heard by Paddy McBay, the despatch manager, who was on a walkabout looking for the packers. The relatively lenient three-day suspension of the four players that followed was said to be because one of the players was Paddy's brother. As the shirt packing was relatively slack after the Christmas rush, the suspensions caused no inconvenience in the despatch department.

Social Events, Rituals and the 'Rattle'

There were, of course, social events in Tillies (as there were in all the factories), such as annual dances and bus outings. In the cutting room, Jack Anthony, a band-knife cutter, organised summer bus outings and Joan Kennedy had a few football/shopping specials to Belfast. In total contrast, there was Dan Doran's bus pilgrimages to Lough Derg, and some laundry workers were known to have taxi-picnic outings to places like Grianan Fort. Of all the bus runs, and as could be expected, Joan's football special to Belfast was the most event-filled, such as the time she 'lost' a passenger and the bus ended up in a farmyard on the way home after the driver took a wrong turn. The lost passenger, George Molloy, a mechanic in the factory, got a lift home in a car, unknown to Joan who spent almost an hour hanging out of the bus shouting: "George Molloy, George Molloy," as it circled Belfast City Hall.

Workers' outing to Donegal in 1940s. (L/R): Ronnie Young (stock-control manager), John Platt (head electrician), Jessie Davis (cutting-room operator), Myra Ferguson, Seamus Mullan (cutter) and Unknown.
(Courtesy Jessie Moore)

Tillies' girls in Belfast for the match. (L/R): Bridie Harkin, Ivy Cassidy and May Parkhill. (Courtesy May Parkhill)

Tillies' football supporters. Three laundry workers in Belfast for Derry City match (L/R): Kathleen Smith, May Parkhill and Hanna Devlin. (Courtesy May Parkhill)

Picnic in Portrush. Standing at back: Eileen Sharkey. Sitting (L/R): Kathleen Breen, Peggy Murray, Unknown, May Parkhill and Sadie Doherty. Sitting at front: Frances Harkin. (Courtesy May Parkhill)

Three lovely lassies from Tillies at Portrush. (L/R): Joanna Dean, Molly Martin and Eithne Duffy. (Courtesy Eithne Glackin)

Workers' outing in 1940s. Included in front row (L/R): Kitty McSherry, Lily McSherry, Sadie Conaghan, Kitty Gallagher and (with coat open) Phyllis Madden. (Courtesy Tom Curran)

Fun at Portrush. Back row (L/R): Bridge Carlin and Unknown. Middle
row (L/R): Kathleen McFeeley and Unknown. Front row (L/R): Mary
Carlin and Mona Kivelehan. (Courtesy Mary Hegarty)

Sitting it out at the Tillies' dance. (L/R): Albert Norris, Rose Gillespie, Mrs
Cauley and husband Charlie and Nellie Graham. (Courtesy Sheila Molloy)

Retirement function for the laundry manageress, held in The Irish Kitchen in Derry (where the Debenham store now stands) in mid-1950s. Front row (L/R): Nellie Shongo, Cissie Kelly (laundry manageress), May Harrigan and Sadie Doherty. Middle row: Unknown, Kathleen Murray, Peggy Murray, Bernie McChrystal, Agnes Moore and Kathleen McLaughlin. Top row: Marie Ramsey, Unknown, Nora Browne, Mary O'Donnell and Unknown. (Courtesy Sadie Morris)

Tillies' staff dance in Broomhill Hotel in 1950s. Seated front row with respective wives (L/R): S Moore (cutting-room manager), M Harkin (Carndonagh factory manager, Co Donegal), S Barber (Foyle factory manager) and B Sherrard (laundry manager). Directly behind Mrs Sherrard are: Eddie Farren (head mechanic), P McBay (stock-room manager and Ross Sherrard (time-study officer). Next to him, on left, is J McNally (despatch manager). (Courtesy Sheila Molloy)

The traditional five minutes stoppage of the speed belt was eventually abandoned by management in favour of extending both the morning and afternoon breaks to fifteen minutes. Tea urns were introduced, complete with trays of white mugs, which were brought up to the different rooms by the hoist. The workers handed in a ticket, which they bought from the forewomen, for the tea. The week's tickets cost one shilling and sixpence ($7\frac{1}{2}$p) at the time, but soon increased in price, to the annoyance of one particular woman, Annie Doyle, who was another personality with her own plan to beat the price rise, as remembered by her co-worker, Kathleen Duffy:

They put up the price of the week's tea to one and sixpence. What does Annie do? She went into Woolworth's and never told anyone what she bought until Monday morning when she says to me, "Go you over and get the tea," and handed me a mug. It was like a po (toilet pot) with a handle on it. We all got our tea out of it, three of us.

Annie always had an eye for value and business, and was one of the main contacts operating the barter system. The system worked to the mutual advantage of both the machinists and the cutters, the latter had to have their privately cut shirts made up, and the machinists had to be compensated. This compensation generally involved cutters giving Annie the makings of a shirt or blouse for her co-operation. This business arrangement was also made with different women throughout the factory who had other enterprises in mind, for there was little cloth waste in the cutting room that the girls couldn't utilise in return for making up the cutters' shirts. They would ask the cutter to 'square off' the waste cuttings in the bins. Then, with their individual talent and ingenuity, they could make patchwork bedroom quilts, flags, bunting, men's handkerchiefs and children's underclothing from the white cloth wastage.

Good fortune was later to smile on Annie Doyle when, as part of a syndicate of five women, she drew a horse in the Irish Hospitals Grand National Sweepstake while holidaying in Bundoran, Co Donegal. And, typical of Annie's placid nature, she was walking along

Making collars and curls. Sitting (L/R): Unknown and Sheila McLaughlin. Standing (L/R): Unknown, Unknown, May Bradley and Charlotte Kivelehan. (Courtesy Margaret and Rose O'Kane)

Foyle Road on the Saturday of the race when a neighbour asked her if she was not watching the race. Annie replied: "I put sixpence (2$^{1}/_{2}$p) each way on it; that's enough." The horse won and Annie collected £10,000 as her share of the £50,000 prize, a fortune by the standards of the time. Annie was later to emigrate to America, where she married and, sadly, died.

It was not all 'sweat and swear' on the speed belt; there was also the singing and sewing of Joan Kennedy's choir (those girls working immediately beside her on the belt). Singing among the girls was a daily occurrence, for the only diversion they had at that time was an hour's blast from the radio in the morning and afternoon. The singing kept the workers happy and it also kept Davy Neely happy. He was heard to remark: "When they're singing they're working."

And, according to Maisie McLaughlin, they worked better: "When you were singing you just seemed to work faster somehow."

On one occasion, Joan's choir, quick to spot Brian Nolan coming into the machine room sporting a new pair of glasses, immediately started to sing the parody: "My eyes are dim, I cannot see, but I have brought my new specs with me."

With the installation of the radio-record player, Joan, for the most part, reduced the performances of the choir in favour of her record collection, and in the process became the scourge of the mechanics' shop where the machine was located. Favourite among her collection was *Danny Boy*, which she was constantly requesting until one day, putting her blonde head into the mechanics' shop, Eddie Farren, the head engineer, bawled out: "No, not *Danny Boy!*"

Not to be put off and quick as a flash, Joan replied: "What about Jim Reeves or Slim Whitman then?" – subtly adding, "...Mr Farren."

He did not like to be called by his first name, Eddie. On one occasion when he was going down the stairs, a young clippie passed him with the greeting: "Yes, Eddie."

He called back: "I don't remember going to school with you; my name is Mr Farren."

Indeed, the broad, winding stairs between the rooms were not for the accident prone, as no-one ever took their time and they were always running either up or down them. Victor Wright, a department manager, was coming down one day at the same time and speed as a wee clippie, her head covered in massive curlers, was coming up. She was unaware of the accepted traffic procedure of going up on the left side and coming down on the left side. The inevitable happened; she dived up on the right side of the staircase. Victor got a face full of curlers, luckily escaping with some minor cuts to his forehead that he covered with plasters. Immediately, and in good factory tradition, the rumour went around that Victor had been head butted by a wee clippie.

On another occasion, Davy Neely was making his way up the staircase. As fate ordained, he didn't use his regular way of ascending by the goods hoist. Anna Quigg from Donemana came rushing down, shouting, "Get out of my way, I'm late for me bus!" and ran smack into Davy. Anna had no idea who Davy was until the next day, when he sacked her, not for running into him, but for sneaking out early – and as a warning to others.

Some girls continued to sneak out occasionally and would use what was generally thought to be the safer route down the back stairs, through the boiler room and down the yard to the freedom of Foyle Road. The route wasn't all that safe, as Eithne Duffy found out the day she decided to sneak out, unaware that Bobby Sherrard, the laundry manager, had discovered her plan. Eithne tells the story:

> One day, a few of us decided to leave early out through the yard, but someone must have talked, for all I heard was: "There's Bobby Sherrard coming!" I hid in the coal shed, but he found me and marched me looking like a coalman through the machine room, probably to let everyone know that the escape route was discovered.

Amazingly, no matter how much the girls were engrossed in their work and listening to the records, they somehow were aware of what was going on around them and could spot any person or situation that merited the traditional 'rattle'. The girls would hammer their machines with scissors or anything else they had, which could be an embarrassing experience for the particular person. Male cutters were always potential victims, should any of them take a shortcut through the machine rooms, wearing something that caught the girls' eyes or if they knew he was dating a particular girl in that room.

One collar room in particular, formerly a pyjama-sewing room, was the most notorious for giving the rattle and was feared by all male employees, as the author was to find out for himself one embarrassing day:

> Walking through the room to deliver some 'recuts' to the forewoman, one girl noticed I was wearing yellow stockings, and walking back down again, I came under the fierce bombardment of the rattle. I was never seen wearing yellow stockings again, nor walking through the pyjama room, for a long time afterwards.

No-one was immune from the rattle, not even the owner of the factory himself, as Bridget Doherty remembers:

Just after the war ended, we all got an extra five pounds in our pay. I can't remember what it was for; it might have been to celebrate the ending of the war, or because we worked hard at all the Admiralty orders during the war. Anyway, old Mr Fawcett came into our machine room one day and he got the loudest rattle I ever heard; I think he didn't know what was happening.

Some of the workers didn't know what was happening either when they discovered one Monday morning after their August holidays that their machines had been painted green. They could only guess that someone in management required hospital treatment, but it was later explained that the green machines were a response to research findings by industrial psychologists. They were suggesting ways to combat the strain of workers engaged in tedious, monotonous and repetitive employment in the wartime munitions factories and the effects of the conveyor-belt systems of production on workers. Apparently, the psychologists were claiming that certain colours had a tranquillising effect and if these were applied, the working environment could induce more contentment, the theory being that a happy worker was a more productive worker.

Music was also seen to have a calming effect and Tillies' workers had one hour of radio, both morning and evening, over the Tannoy system, the highlight being *Workers Playtime*. Indeed on one occasion, all the factories were invited to a live performance of *Workers Playtime* in the Strand Cinema (now the Multiplex) presented by the show host Wilfred Pickles. His guest on that occasion was Ann Shelton.

Most of the city's large factories got their share of army, navy and air force shirt orders during the war years, and some of the girls took this opportunity to send notes to the forces along with the shirts. When these shirts were ready, they were not individually put in shirt bags but tied in bundles and put into parcels to be sent to the relevant government department. Before they were parcelled, some girls would slip a note into the pocket of a shirt with their name and address. The note would be short and to the point: "If you're single, drop us a line; if you're married, never mind."

One of Tillies' laundry workers did get an answer from a soldier serving in Burma and she continued the correspondence. She recalls:

> I sent him some newspapers, sweets and toothpaste. Dan Doran would parcel them up for me out in the despatch. We arranged to meet after the war and I went over to the Waterside station to meet him. He stayed ten days in our house and we stayed just good friends. His mother later wrote to thank me for befriending her son during the war.

If the rattle was an embarrassing experience, the ritual carried out on those getting married was a more terrifying one. It was almost impossible for those girls leaving to get married to slip out unnoticed, because it generally was their close friends who tipped off the other workers. The unfortunate girl had to grin-and-bear the ordeal, which typically involved getting painted with lipstick and tied up with all sorts of coloured ribbons, head to toe. They were then put into a large wicker basket with wheels and pushed around the entire room, after which they would be taken outside the factory and tied to the public toilet railings at the foot of Tillies' steps. With the construction, at a later time, of a water fountain roundabout at the John Street end of the bridge, the bride-to-be would be put into it.

Phyllis Moran, about to get married to one of the cutters, relates her own experience:

> They tied my coat up with ribbons – no, not really ribbons but bits of cloth cut up like ribbons. It took me nearly a couple of hours to get them off to go home. Then they started to carry me from the room I worked in down to the cutting room where John was, and I got very nervous with them for doing this and I battered and thumped them. There was one wee girl near me, I didn't know who she was, she had lovely blonde hair and I grabbed her by the hair and nearly pulled it out of her. It was terrible. You didn't know what they would do next.

Bridie Cooke (née McCloskey) had a less frightening, though more embarrassing, experience:

I was able to get out of the factory without any fuss because I had left work a few days before and was walking home when the rain came on. I put up my umbrella and was showered with shirt buttons. The girls had stuffed them into the umbrella, the people on the street didn't know what had happened, and I could do nothing but blush and hurry on.

Though the ritual was frightening, all was forgotten at 'the big night' when the bride-to-be was given her wedding present from the workers, which was generally a very practical gift. Usually, these gifts would have been bed linen, a lemonade jug and glasses, pillow sets or a box of cutlery. But most popular were the tea sets, with some girls claiming to have got as many as three and four tea sets as wedding presents. The actual wedding-day festivities were not too long-drawn-out, as Berna McDermott recalls:

The thing that amazed me in those days was that a girl was able to get married, have her photo taken, be at the reception and still catch the three o'clock train at the GNR station for Dublin. Then, as the train sounded the whistle and slowly passed Tillies, all the girls would hang out of the windows on the Foyle Road side, waving and shouting.

Going to Dublin was big at the time; it would not be an exaggeration to say that most Derry factory girls would not have got to see Dublin except on their honeymoon or, as Stella McDaid put it: "Dublin was another world; Buncrana was most people's limit."

The cutters getting married were generally able to spot the danger signs and were alert to all the moves going on behind the scenes, thereby well prepared to take evasive action, or so the author thought:

I decided to leave at lunchtime and was halfway down the stairs when three girls came after me. I ran as fast as I could along Foyle Road and down the Quay. At the Guildhall, they were still running after me, shouting and screaming, much to the amusement of onlookers. I eventually got home and fell asleep with exhaustion on the sofa. I never thought women could run as fast as that.

Another cutter was trapped up in the attic rooms by four girls who threatened to take his trousers off if he did not come with them for the ritual. The cutter took emergency action: "Hold on, girls, I'll do it for you." As he proceeded to unbuckle his belt, and with his trousers halfway down, the women fled.

A number of marriages were made in Tillies during the period 1945-75. Two despatch clerks, one trainee manager, one stockroom assistant, one mechanic and three cutters all married girls who worked in Tillies, and there were probably more marriages throughout the entire history of the factory.

Accidents, Lotteries and the Chocolate Bonus

Accidents at Tillies were not that common, but all the women were vulnerable to one frightening experience – the possibility of getting a needle through their finger. The more modern and faster the sewing machines became, the greater the risk there was of the girls' fingers being caught by the needle. It was an occupational hazard and a very painful experience, which brought with it the less-than-sympathetic remark, often made to the unfortunate girl by her co-workers: "You'll never be a machinist until you get the needle in your finger."

The real hazard was not so much the needle *sticking* into the finger as actually *breaking* in the finger. If a needle became stuck in the finger, then the injured worker could turn the pulley wheel backwards and painfully withdraw the needle herself. If the needle should break in her finger, a mechanic was called to remove the needle with a pair of fine pliers. One particular machinist had a more terrifying experience, as Mary Hegarty (née McAllister), a service worker in charge of a conveyer belt, remembers:

> One day, Margaret Feeney, who had lovely long blonde hair, was leaning over her machine when her hair got caught and tangled up in the wheel. She was in a terrible state, crying and very frightened. Some girl was quick thinking and turned off the whole belt and we were able to gently cut some of her lovely hair off and free her. But it was a terrible experience for her; it was the first and last of that kind of accident ever happening.

The male cutters also had the occupational hazard of cutting their fingers while operating the band knife, the danger being equally possible using the smaller, mobile motor-driven straight knife used for cutting the bulk shirts on the cutting table. And similar to the girl machinists, there was the traditional belief expressed by the more experienced cutters: "You'll never be a cutter until you cut your finger." At times, it was not the wisest or the safest comment to make, especially if the top of the unfortunate cutter's finger was lying beside the band knife, which was the case of one Joe Callan. Over the years, Tillies' band-knife and straight-knife cutters had their share of cuts. Indeed, the author almost lost his life working for Tillies, though not at the cutting:

> The incident happened during a postal strike in early 1971, when Paddy McBay, the despatch clerk, asked me if I would use my car to take a letter confirming acceptance of a M&S order to catch the one o'clock plane out of Belfast, as the jobs of the girls depended on it. With a stupid sense of importance, I envisaged myself as the Pony Express rider in the cowboy pictures. The mail had to get through, and I put my boot to the floor. Approaching Toome, I heard what I thought was the sound of a flat tyre. So, stopping the car, I had a look, but all appeared okay. So I continued, speeding, when just before approaching the M1 motorway, I met a series of bends in the road and a large lorry in front. Faced with the decision whether to slow down, which would cost me precious time, or overtake, I luckily slowed down and immediately the car lurched on one side and sparks appeared before the windscreen.
>
> I managed to control the vehicle to a stop. Getting out, I found that there were only three wheels on the car, and despite a search up and down the road, under the car and in fields, the missing wheel could not be found. I thumbed a lift back to Toome and informed the police of what had happened and the dangerous position of the car on the road. They assured me they would take charge of the situation and permitted me to continue to Belfast Airport.
>
> I got the letter delivered on time and returned to the police station, thanks to a succession of lifts, and was told my car was repaired and could be collected from the garage around the corner. On my way out of the station, I called back to the policeman to ask where he found the missing wheel: "You would never have found it, sir. It was up a tree, and you must have been breaking speed limits for the wheel to bounce up a tree." I thanked him, getting quickly out of the police station and glad to be driving home, all the time keeping my eye on the speedometer and the rear mirror.

The more immediate material and social needs of the girls were supplied through the unique factory culture of lotteries and clubs. The lotteries gave them access to a lump sum of money and through the clubs, women could have a hair perm, portrait photo taken, or new shoes and clothes. A lottery draw could be run by anyone in the factory, provided they could recruit a reliable number of girls to pay a certain amount of money over a certain number of weeks for an agreed amount of pay-out money. Lotteries could be extended over five, ten, fifteen or twenty weeks, with payouts varying from five pounds to twenty pounds, depending on the popular demand. Numbers would be put into a container, with each member of the lottery syndicate drawing out a number that indicated their payout week ie, first, second, and so on. The organiser generally had the number one draw as of right, or if preferred, the last week, depending on the needs or requirements of the particular organiser.

There were various reasons for women starting a lottery, as Margaret Nellis, a front stitcher, explains: "It might be a personal emergency, like covering First Communion expenses, and some girls who drew low numbers would ask those girls who drew the high numbers to switch because they could not wait for the money."

Maisie McLaughlin gave a more practical reason: "It was a good way of getting a rise." And for others, like Phil McLaughlin, a mechanic, the lottery was a way to achieve his personal ambition to become a trumpet player. Probably influenced by the showbands at the beginning of the '60s, Phil decided he would buy a trumpet and learn to play it. So he organised a twenty-week lottery and promptly bought the trumpet with his first week's draw. However, with a twenty-week draw, there was always the possibility of payment fatigue and Phil almost had the trumpet learned when the last week's payout was made. He never organised another twenty-week lottery ever again. And it's very likely that the other apprentice mechanic, George Kilkie, who finally got his last draw, probably never took another lottery draw either.

Agents in the factory ran clubs for some of the city shops. Operating on the hire-purchase system of weekly payments, the agent would give a signed note for a certain amount of money to the particular person to take to the shop. The photo clubs were very popular primarily because cameras were expensive for a factory girl to buy and seen as something of a luxury item. Having a photo portrait taken was also very expensive and there was a practice in the factory of several girls sharing the cost of the club, as Eithne Duffy recalls: "Me and Theresa McMonagle took the club between us. It was like about a shilling (5p) each a week for, I think, twenty weeks. We got three photos each from Leslie Stuart." To have one's photo taken by Leslie Stuart was a status symbol in those days, since he was a highly acclaimed photographer. The financial cost of the week's various business transactions was made accountable on pay day.

Friday afternoon in Tillies was like a money-exchange market as debts were paid and collections made. The different lottery and club organisers could be seen moving frantically through the machine rooms, looking for, and collecting from, their clients. Others would be seen collecting for churches and charities, for the 'giving culture' had a strong tradition among the Derry factory girls. In Tillies, Florrie Logue never missed a Friday collecting for the Foreign Missions, while St Martin and St Anthony had their supporters, who rattled their empty snuff tins or the empty cardboard button boxes at everybody. Also, once a month, various girls would collect money for flowers for the Forty Hours Devotion in their particular parishes. Maisie McLaughlin recalls: "We always collected for the Nazareth House and sent the wanes selection boxes at Christmas and chocolate eggs at Easter, and some girls would bring in real eggs instead of the chocolate ones."

Lottery organisers, debt collectors and union shop stewards collecting their subscriptions had to be quick off the mark on Fridays, for some girls would be finished with their amounts and leave early, forgetting to pay, whereas some others, of course, would not be at their work. This would result in a short lottery payout that particular week, and what happened then is explained by one woman who had the experience:

> The woman running the lottery would say to you: "Look, so-and-so owes you ten bob (50p) but she told me she would pay you on Monday."

Periods of short-time working – when the girls had to sign on the bru (the local labour exchange) for a few days each week – presented the most problems for the club agents. Some agents, though, were very resilient and responded to the situation by taking up sentinel duty inside the bru on Thursday, the day the girls got their dole money. One agent would be standing on the middle of the stairs, and you didn't get past her, and she knew exactly who had to pay and she never left those stairs until she got paid.

Temporary and permanent signing on the bru was becoming more regular as the shirt industry in Derry began to be more vulnerable to increasing foreign imports, the ups and downs of sales in the home markets as well as the rapidly changing styles and materials of fashion shirts.

Undoubtedly, the city's shirt industry was facing a crisis and it was recognised that shirt making had to become more efficient and economic. Significantly, Tillies' head office in Chester appointed an Englishman, Stephen Barber, in 1953 as factory manager. He was the first Englishman to be appointed to a managerial position in Tillies. It was said at the time that he was very good at figures and economics; and together with Davy Neely, who knew the factory game inside out, big changes in the fortunes of Tillies were expected. Indeed, it was during Barber's tenure that Tillies' sewing and singing factory girl was to be moulded into a more efficient and economic worker. The consequences of such were to traumatically transform life in Tillies.

Not very long after his arrival in Tillies, Barber took what could be seen as his first rather humorous initiative to increase production when he promised a section of machinists a box of chocolates if they achieved a certain target. Reminiscing about it later, Berna McDermott (née McShane) could see the long-term implications of the so-called 'chocolate bonus'. She puts it into perspective: "The idea was that once you hit your target, it proved you could do it. It was a trap, and they would say if you were able to do it one day, then you could do it every day."

The box of chocolates ploy was also put into perspective by Stella McDaid: "What sort of a box did you think it was? It wasn't a big box tied with a colour ribbon and a big bow in the middle. It was a wee half-pound box. Anyway, it didn't last long and not many got it."

To encourage punctuality and attendance, another innovation was the introduction of time-clock cards, with all the workers having to 'clock in' both morning and evening. Any card without the incriminating red mark, which denoted late clocking, would be put into a draw for a fortnight's foreign holiday. The venture had a small measure of success, and although the draw was eventually abandoned, the time-clock system remained and became very much part of the beat-the-clock life in Tillies.

Although that particular section of machinists had no taste for the chocolate bonus, Barber decided on a factory-wide initiative to achieve better and more efficient production figures, so signalling the phasing-out of the conveyor belts. He introduced an ambitious new approach that involved each floor becoming a self-contained production unit, complete with cutting, laundry and machining facilities. All the front stitching for the entire factory was now located in a separate area of the fourth-floor machine room rather than on the speed belts. Roisin Gallagher describes the situation:

> All the fronts were stitched in our room, and when they were finished, we took them and put them on a big table at the end of the room. Then Sadie Conaghan would count them and tie them in bundles, and other service girls from the different rooms would come and collect them.

However, the idea of a factory all on the one floor was ahead of its time, even for Tillies in the twentieth century, particularly as the internal structure of the building was seen as totally unsuitable. A single-floor factory idea did take hold at a different time and at a different location.

Time Study Engineering Changes All

In the early 1960s, a new approach to production was beginning to take hold. Originally called Time Study Engineering (TSE), it later became known among the girls as 'time and motion' or 'time study'.

One of the city's other large shirt factories, Hogg and Mitchell, had already introduced this latest production method, with its proven record to lower costs and increase production significantly. This was also just what Tillies was looking for. Also, M&S was requiring more efficiency from all its suppliers. So, in 1963, a company called the Consortium of Organised Consultants was employed and TSE was introduced into Tillies.

For some girls, life in Tillies was to become traumatic; for others it was seen as the arrival of *The Good Ship Lollipop*, for rumour had it that good money could be earned. The laundry department was the obvious first choice for this experiment with TSE. There were fewer operations there than in the machine rooms and the latest German technology, the Kanniegeser, an automatic smoothing machine, had been installed. More importantly, the laundry workers had a 'bonus mentality', for the laundry was the only department in the entire factory operating a bonus system, as May Parkhill remembers:

> We were on our own time; we got paid by the dozen. I think it was about a shilling (5p) or something, I am not sure, but I do know we were well enough paid. You could work at your own speed and have the odd wee chat. There was no set amount for you to do, though those on just the flat wage would be told occasionally to increase their effort.

In the laundry, the floor plan was somewhat similar to the way the girls on the conveyor belt worked at the time, with up to eight smoothers facing each other on both sides of a long table using gas irons that were both smelly and heavy. The big difference between the two was that smoothers had to stand on their feet all day, which had a painful effect, as Sadie Morris explains:

You were standing all day long, sometimes in high heels, and by the time you got home, your feet were burnt off you, especially sometimes when you had to work till nine at night. You hadn't to work in if you didn't want to, but if you refused, well, you were seen as not pulling your weight, you know what I mean?

To facilitate TSE, the ground plan of the laundry was restructured and the long benches replaced by smaller ones that had only two smoothers, and several of those were placed around the Kanniegeser. This was because the Kanniegeser could only smooth the front and back body of the shirt, which meant that the cuffs and collars had to be smoothed by the iron. And by this time, the gas irons had been replaced with electric ones, equally heavy though not as smelly. These new irons had to be handled with much more care because, apart from the possibility of a severe burn, there was another hazard, as Sadie explains:

You had to be very careful that the iron was at the right heat or you would singe the shirt, or worse, when the nylon shirts came, you could take a lump out of them. The nylon would stick to the hot iron, and many a singed shirt Cissie Kelly, the laundry supervisor, would find, and then all hell broke loose, because she was a very strict supervisor.

Within a relatively short time, TSE was completely operational in the laundry room, and next, the engineers moved into the machine rooms, where their task was to be more contentious and controversial.

The machine rooms could be said to be the heart and soul of life in Tillies, if only for the reason that the majority of women in the factory worked there. That situation was about to be irreversibly changed, most noticeably by innovations in the factory layout.

The familiar machine-room characteristic of long lines of women working shoulder to shoulder and facing each other across the bench disappeared along with the conveyor belts. The new ground plan of the machine rooms was similar to a classroom formation, with the women working behind and abreast of each other in their own individual work areas – each clearly defined with floor markings. Then, with the girls isolated and corralled in their own individual work space, they underwent close scrutiny of their working technique by the work-study engineer, who attempted to set a time for the completion of the particular operation. In practice, the engineer, almost always complete with clipboard and stopwatch, would take up a position close beside the operator. Then her every movement would be timed and recorded. His basic task was to eliminate any unnecessary time-wasting actions and bad working habits that the operator may have developed, and by so doing, the work-study recommendations would make her a more efficient and productive worker.

This procedure of timing a shirt-factory worker was understandably a tense and uncomfortable experience for the particular girl, despite the engineer's request that she 'just work normally', which meant little to Eithne Duffy, a fitter:

> It was nerve-racking. The time-study man would tell you just to work as normal and steady, and you sat and just went round the work at your normal speed, but they would turn round and say to you, "I know you can go quicker than that."

Some girls could, of course, work faster than others; and it was this question of mixed ability that puzzled and worried Berna McShane, a hemmer:

> None of us were the same, so how could they say that all the sideseamers were able to do this amount and all the front stitchers could do that amount? Maybe two or three could do it, but there were another ten or so who couldn't. They set the amounts for what they wanted; all they wanted was for one girl to do the amounts, then they would argue everyone should do them.

It appeared that management mistrust had not melted away with the chocolate bonus but still persisted, which one engineer, Michael Lynch, appeared to confirm as he explained the 'solution' to the question of mixed ability:

All girls would not have the same ability or aptitude towards work. There would be four or five girls doing the same job and each would have their own way of doing their work, so the first thing to do was to establish a method for doing the job. Then, with each doing the operation with the same method, a standard time was set. Some could not achieve the times, but there was always one girl who could. So that one girl proved that the time could be achieved.

With his initial timing of the girl completed, the engineer would leave to do his calculations, and return with a provisional time for the job. This time was generally described as 'loose', but since it was only provisional, the engineer would return at a later date to repeat his observations and establish a 'tighter' permanent time for the job on the argument and assumption that the girl had become more efficient since she was last timed. Those workers who had serious difficulty with the permanent times or, in the jargon of time study, 'under-achieving operators', would, according to Lynch, receive further attention from the engineers:

> We would go along to these people to see where they were wasting time and tell them: "Look, you've done that for the first hour, now your target for the second hour is to equal that, or try and maybe get a wee bit better." I would try and show them that under-achieving was sometimes a mental block – if they think they can't do it, they will never do it. Sometimes it was necessary to make a slight adjustment to the rate to keep them happy.

The workers were far from happy, because the setting of permanent times (and their acceptance by the workers) was certainly a contentious and controversial issue. The unions for their part would often contest the times and bring in their own time-study men to re-time some of the operations. So, the subsequent negotiations among unions, management and the workers became a very protracted process, though time study itself seemed inevitable, as Berna McShane pointed out during a union meeting: "I said we really didn't want it, it's not fair, and the work's doubled. But the union said you can't stop progress, and that meant that time and study was in, whether the girls wanted it or not."

The work rates certainly had doubled, as another worker commented: "On the speed belt, we had to do forty-eight dozen a day. But that was between two of us. Now it was forty-eight dozen for one girl. How did that happen?"

One worker, who remembers asking an engineer that particular question, recalls with understandable sarcasm his reply:

> They would say to us: "We're going to provide you with work aids, new machines, new this, new that. The work will be flowing and you'll have no problems. Blah, blah, blah, etc." But it all boiled down to this – they took us for a sleigh ride and we were stupid, so we were.

A variety of work aids did appear, and they're best described by one of the girls who had to work them:

Smiles on the conveyor belt. Included: Anna McDaid, Gladys Fraser, Annie Burke, Josie Doherty, Alice Walsh, Maisie Bonner, Stella McDaid and Margaret Callaghan. (Courtesy George Sweeney)

I remember they made a whole lot of wooden horses to hold the work, and the mechanics fitted a lever under the machine table that you hit with your thigh and the guide lifted up instead of you having to lift it up with your hand. And the wee gadget that you pressed and the machine back-stitched without us having to turn the work backwards and then forward again.

Admittedly, these aids did help the girls work more efficiently, though making up their wages didn't become any easier. And a whole series of new phrases of industrial jargon was entering the factory-floor vocabulary, such as underachieving, overachieving, standard rate, special rate, waiting time, special time and degree of difficulty. The girls now had little time for singing or giving the rattle. Here are a few of their comments about that time:

We were killed for our money, we didn't get the money for what we put out; it was very unfair . . .

You hadn't time to bless yourself never mind sing. The speed belt used to be a holiday camp, for no matter what happened, your wages were steady . . .

If you didn't work hard, you had little wages with the time and motion.

Under TSE, every worker was now aware, if they were not before, of just how many minutes were in a working day as they totalled up their work tickets. What was important now to the girls was counting up their work tickets at the end of the day to see how many 'standard minutes' they had totalled. Stella McDaid, a cuffer, complained: "Tickets were just your life. They meant everything to you, sticking or sewing them onto your sheet and then when you counted them at dinner-time you would say to yourself, dear God, I thought I had more than that."

It was often the case that a girl could have her work sheet completely filled with tickets and yet barely reach her total standard minutes for the day, which at the time was 550 and indicated that the girl was working at 100%. By contrast, other girls would have their work sheet only partly filled and be over the total standard minutes that qualified them for bonus payments, the amount of bonus depending how much over the 100% they were working. This apparent unfairness resulted from the process by which the fast worker would have had the choice of the different bundles of work to be done. These bundles of work were carried from the cutting room to large tables in the machine rooms by such service women as Florrie Logue, Peggy Brady, Mary McAllister, Clare Donnelly and Olive Fleming, to mention but a few. There would be large bundles, small bundles, big sizes and small sizes, depending on the particular order and the way it was cut and bundled in amounts by the cutting department.

If the cutting room had no problems with the shading of the material, then the bundles of work would be large; but if there were few rolls of material the same shade, then the bundles could be very small indeed. Also, the size range of most shirt orders would extend from the very small size through the medium to the large and extra large and, consequently, you could have large bundles of the smaller-sized work and small bundles of the larger-sized work. All bundles were tied in units of dozens, which was the standard unit of amount, and some of the large bundles could have anything between five and ten dozen. By contrast, the smaller bundles might only have a fraction of a dozen. The work tickets would be attached to the bundle of work and would indicate the amount in dozens and the number of minutes allowed to complete the bundle. Each girl would lift a bundle as she required, and there would be some disagreements and differences of opinion. One supervisor recalls: "Now that's when there were rows in the factory. Oh my God, every day in the week there was a row."

As TSE became established, controversy and competition increasingly became part of life in Tillies:

At the start it was a bit of an affliction, all diving about getting their amounts. It was because they were afraid they wouldn't get their money, that they wouldn't make a wage at the end of the week. Time study worked on the girls' fear. You always got the one who went down and got the big bundles, but you would some-times get the person who would say, "Well, my last bundle was big, so you take that one now." Size 17 was always last and all the size 14$^{1/2}$ and 15 were all gone.

With the smaller bundles came the added annoyance of having to constantly change the colour of thread, and that really slowed the machinist. Complaining about the effect on earnings that this chang-ing of colours was having brought no real sympathy from the time-study people: "When you told them you would need extra time for all the changing of the thread, they blinded us with science and they would show you the clipboard and say, 'It's allowed for; there it is in black and white.'"

Some girls chased the money, working at over 100%, and they fared well. Some did not, but instead completed the required mini-mum of 550 standard minutes that qualified them for the basic wage; some others worked the 'dead horses' system. This meant that some girls would put tickets on their daily time sheet for work they had not done, so the next day they had to work harder. Playing the dead hors-es was a dangerous gamble for any girl, as Eithne Duffy recalls:

> I remember the department manager Brian Nolan was standing behind me and my basket was full to the brim with 'dead horses', and the sweat was lashing off me and I was ready to cry because I was thinking, *How am I going to get these finished before half five the night?* So I finally told him that I wasn't going to get them finished, so he said, "Well, that's all right." But then you had to go in early the next morning, or instead of taking your dinner break, work it.

This contrasted greatly with playing 'catch up' on the conveyer belt system with the comradeship among the girls: "When you were on the belt, if your machine broke down or you were stuck, the other girls could have helped you, but once you went on time study they couldn't, for they had to earn their own money."

It became more difficult to bring the dead horses to life when the dinner break was reduced from one and a quarter hours to a half-hour

A crowded canteen table. Front row (L/R): Unknown, Isobel Breslin, Kathleen McAdams, Maureen Cooper and Gladys Fraser. Middle row (L/R): Annie Burke, Stella McDaid, Annie Coyle and Unknown. Back row (L/R): Unknown and Alice Walsh. (Courtesy George Sweeney)

Brian Nolan (department manager) is surrounded by workers in the canteen. (Courtesy George Sweeney)

as a result of an agreement between management and unions for the girls to work up time to facilitate the closure of the factory on Friday afternoons. This was made possible because of the introduction of the canteen. In many respects, the girls now became captive workers, for, being in Tillies all day, they missed their run home at lunch break, though some must have had to run very fast, as one girl said: "We went back up to Creggan at dinner-time, come hail, rain or snow, because we got over an hour at that time. It was a rush but it was good to get out home in the middle of the day."

The canteen was a poor substitute for home cooking because, though it meant less for the rats, with fewer crumbs around the machine rooms, it certainly had no à la carte menu for the workers. There was no such thing as a hot meal, though if anyone had a sausage roll with them, it could be heated. There was also a tuck shop with sweets and chocolate. There was no tick in the canteen, so the selling of confectionery did not threaten Charlie Cauley's business or the apple-tart trade. Basically, the canteen was a re-organisation of the tea urns from the various rooms to the one location, and everyone still had to queue with ticket in hand for the white mug of tea. Because of the canteen limitations, there were two sittings in the morning, 9.30 and 10.15, and then a three o'clock sitting in the afternoon, which was poorly attended. Smoking, with the usual 'pass the butt' ritual, was allowed in the canteen.

It was possible, though not very likely, that some of the dead horses could be done while a girl was on 'waiting time'. Under an in-built agreement of time study, everyone was allowed to incorporate any time spent idly waiting for work, for whatever reason, into their day's total minute tally. The situation of a machinist sitting idle generally resulted from two main causes: either the girl could not locate a mechanic to repair her machine or work was badly cut. Any such work was rebundled and returned to the cutting room, and the girl who returned the work would clock off and go on waiting time, which was paid at a lower rate and was frowned upon by the supervisors who were under orders to keep waiting time to a minimum.

From a management viewpoint, waiting time was not to be tolerated and, consequently, anyone clocking off was quizzed, questioned

Time out for a photograph. (L/R): Olive Fleming, Unknown, Josie Doherty (supervisor) and Mrs McFadden (supervisor). (Courtesy George Sweeney)

A crowded mechanics' shop in Tillies. Mechanics (L/R): Seamus McLaughlin, George Molloy and Paul Doherty (head only), Charlie McLaughlin and Terry McLaughlin. Woman at front: Maureen Cooper, then (L/R): Alice Walsh (partly hidden), Unknown, Gladys Fraser, Isobel Breslin and Annie Burke. (Courtesy Charlie McLaughlin and George Sweeney)

117

and queried as to her reason: "They watched us like a hawk and we were questioned all the time by the supervisor, who'd say, 'What are you clocking off for?' And when you said your machine was broke she would say, 'Is the mechanic coming out?'"

Waiting for a mechanic to fix her machine was a more frequent occurrence for the girls, particularly since mechanics did not operate under any time-study or bonus system. They would not have been inconvenienced by any excessive demands put on them, apart from the pressure by department managers to repair the machines quickly. It was very much in the interest of the machinist not to antagonise the mechanic:

> If you were in with them, you were all right, and you had to be in with them. You couldn't fall out with them. They had the upper hand, they called the tune and they could take all day. Sometimes they would say, "This has to be fixed in the mechanics' shop." And they would bring you a spare machine, and the girls didn't like working with a strange machine. You had to get used to it.

Indeed, not only had the girls to cope with these trials and tribulations of the working day, they also had to resign themselves to the ongoing, changing life and working relationships in Tillies that the introduction of TSE had inflicted. Life in Tillies was also about to change for the cutting-room staff.

All the various different reports and rumours about time study were filtering through to the cutting room, and when it eventually arrived, nobody knew what to expect. What we did know for certain was that a change in working practices was inevitable and that the carefree atmosphere and outlooks within the cutting room were about to end. It was a working atmosphere I had enjoyed ever since I first climbed up Tillies' steps back in 1950 as a young, frightened and excited boy of fifteen years.

I walked down them twenty-two years later as a more frightened and frustrated unemployed married man. The person who was with me that first day and every day until he retired was my next-door neighbour, Willie 'Ginger' Quinn. Willie had to take compulsory retirement in 1965 after working in Tillies for fifty years. He did not qualify for redundancy payment and at that time a golden handshake had not yet become part of industrial ethics. He did, however, receive what could be described as a 'copper handshake' of one hundred pounds, or two pounds for each of his fifty years of loyalty!

In Tillies, I learned all the attributes that were thought to make you an adult at that time: smoking, swearing, gambling, borrowing, noticing girls, which went with the job, and also learning to dance. The dancing tuition was given by Willie 'Duke' Doran, the fastest band-knife cutter in Tillies, if not in Derry. I felt I had to learn, as some girls reported that I was a wallflower at the dances. With the aid of a domestic two-handled bin that was used for rags, Willie told me to put one hand around the bin and catch the handle with the other hand, then he started counting: "One, two, three. One, two, three," while showing me the steps and at the same time whistling an old dance tune *The Cuckoo Waltz*. The swinging sixties, of course, made old-time dancing out of date and put me back on the wall, but Joan Kennedy was quick to teach me to jive like the Yanks at the Embassy.

Such a prospect of change in the cutting room, with the introduction of TSE, created feelings of anxiety and apprehension that were heightened whenever the cutting-room manager, Sammy Moore, was said to have remarked to one of the cutting staff: "Wally's no dozer." This was a reference to the ability of a time-study engineer by the name of Wallace, who was attached to the Kurt Salmon Group – then carrying out the study. What this was taken to imply was that Wallace would not and could not be easily hoodwinked by any tricks of the trade, and henceforth, wages would be earned by the sweat of the brow, as indeed all rumours verified. All this was worrying, for sweat was hard to find on anyone's brow in the cutting room, though we did what was expected from us. The only accountability in relation to a fair day's pay for a fair day's work that existed in the cutting room was a notebook into which everyone had to record daily performances. Then every morning, Tom McDaid, the foreman cutter, would transfer all the notebook data into his master ledger.

This accountability had more to do with work in progress than it had with who worked harder than whom. Nobody was ever questioned about performance by the cutting-room manager. Nor had it to do with any bonus payments, for everyone was on a basic wage, and the prospect of earning more wages under time study was received with a lot of scepticism by some and anticipation by others. The sceptics thought we were all going to be put on the chain gangs, whereas others thought we would earn enough to be wearing gold chains around the neck. Neither was to be the case. What did transpire was similar to the controversy and competition that happened in the machine rooms. Some cutters chased the money and some did not, but in any case, life in Tillies was to be irreversibly changed for the cutters.

Before the arrival of Wally, all the pros and cons of timing people in the cutting room were constantly debated and discussed in the men's parlour, generally under the chairmanship of Jim Crawford, chain-smoking his Gallaher Blues and with everyone having their say-so. I remember making this point: "Never mind the degree of difficulty, what about the degree of danger? You'll never cut yourself with a pencil or tying a knot." With regard to us band-knife cutters, that was a particular bone of contention, and used later as a bargaining chip for contesting the times set by Wallace, though such opinions did not influence him.

When it eventually was my turn to be timed and I inquired from Wallace about the degree of danger, he agreed and assured me it was incorporated in the overall timing, the same line that had been used on the girls. Subsequently, every process in the cutting room was timed: shading, spreading, pencilling, tying up, making samples, straight-knife cutting and band-knife cutting. And with all grievances debated and discussed between management, worker and unions, the cutting room also entered the modern time-study era of production.

Band-knife men and the straight-knife cutters (these were the men who cut the larger parts of the shirt on the spreading table) were paid according to the number of shirt lengths they cut, and in the case of the former, at what depth. A shirt length incorporated all the component parts that made up the shirt, and the depth was calculated in the number of plies of the material rather than in the then-standard unit – a dozen. All this information was detailed on the work sheet. There was a governing depth at which the shirts were allowed to be cut by the band-knife men. For example, if it were stipulated at 130 plies then, in the sample below, size 15$^{1}/_{2}$ would have to be halved before being cut.

Size:	14$^{1}/_{2}$	15	15$^{1}/_{2}$	16
Quantity:	80	120	150	75

The cutter would, of course, get twice the time for cutting any size that had to be halved. He could be tempted not to halve the work and gain time but at the risk of his work being returned as badly cut. Then he'd lose time repairing it and since time cost money, the blame game was played by everyone when it came to any interruptions or delays, and in this respect, the tolerance level of the machinists with badly cut work was nil. When such work was returned to the cutting room, a nerve-racking ritual would take place for the band-knife cutters.

The full-length glass doors of the cutting room would swing open, and Brian Nolan, Wesley Parkes or Vera McConnell would appear with a bundle of work over their arms. They would stand looking for Sammy Moore and wait until he would come; then both would march down the room to Jim Crawford who was something of a 'tally man'. It was Jim who consulted his ready reckoner and marked the allotted time that the cutter was allowed on the particular work ticket. Then, when the work was cut and bundled ready for the machine rooms, the ticket would be returned to Crawford for safe-keeping with the name of the cutter on it.

All this time, I would be keeping an eye, as were the other men, on the action. It was certainly an anxious time, watching Crawford thumbing his way through his library of used work sheets and then handing Sammy the incriminating one. At this stage, I would watch Sammy out of the side of my eye as he returned, marching up towards the band knives, hoping he would pass me by; sometimes he did and other times he did not. On those occasions that he did stop at my machine, it was somewhat embarrassing. Nothing was said, he just showed me the fault and walked away and you could almost hear him think, *Well, if you had halved your work as you were supposed to do, you wouldn't have to spend the next half-hour fixing it.*

Sammy never insisted that repairs be done immediately; he knew the supervisors would return to put the pressure on with their usual remark: "We're waiting on that work to complete the order," and would stand beside you until the work was repaired. At this stage, depending on who the particular supervisor was, I would try and sweet talk her into coming back at a later time, as this meant that I could repair the damage while at the same time doing my own work. This would minimise the cost of 'lost time', and there was also the possibility that I could be on waiting time, when they could be repaired at no cost to myself. Of course there would be serious consequences for me if Sammy caught on to it; waiting time was also a controversial and contentious issue in the cutting room.

No-one wanted large amounts of waiting time anyway, because this had the effect of greatly reducing the overall wages for the particular day, irrespective of how fast you had worked previously. The ideal situation was to incorporate small amounts of waiting time into the working day, which had the effect of helping earnings, particularly in the case of difficult work. This strategy was achieved by keeping an eye on the 'carters' to see how soon they'd be finished carting the next lay of shirts to be cut. Then I would put a spurt on to be finished what I was working at so as to be ahead of them. I would then clock off and go on waiting time, all of which was legitimate, or as Wally would put it, "Showing personal initiative and endeavour."

Like machinists, some cutting staff, male and female, chased the money and some did not. But all experienced that sense of urgency, and the changed working relationships, and the at-times tense atmosphere, all of which permeated the cutting room and the entire factory under work-study engineering.

The female cutters' job got more involved under time study and became more of an all-through operation, where previously they would have only performed the one single task, such as shading, or tying up the cut work, or spreading the material. Now they had to shade the cloth before spreading it from the carts and then tie up all the component parts of the shirts in work bundles for the machine rooms after the cutter had finished the cutting.

Indeed, so anxious were they to make safe their wages that some would be waiting to take the work out of the straight-knife cutter's hand as soon as he had it cut and would get the table cleared to start spreading again. Also, some band-knife men, myself included, could also be seen standing waiting to grab the work as soon as it became available from the spreading table. Such was the sense of urgency at times that some of the carters could be seen almost running up the spreading table with the cart and the material fluttering like a flag behind. The woman following the cart had the more difficult time trying to catch the cloth and keep it even on the table; otherwise the cutter who had to cut it would complain that the work was not even enough for cutting and could claim waiting time.

Redundancies and Closure

With the entire factory now working under TSE, an apparently appreciative board of directors re-called Stephen Barber at the end of 1965 to Chester and appointed him Production Director of the entire Tillie and Henderson group of companies. Barber, a mild-mannered but persuasive man, could be said to have transformed life in Tillies, though it must be said that he did so at a social cost among the workforce, which had lost some of its togetherness, in order to gain production figures. It was inevitable that redundancies would occur, since the overall objective of TSE was to achieve a smaller, more efficient and economic workforce to compete against the cheaper imports.

The social cost and effects of TSE were acknowledged by Seamus Quinn, the local branch secretary of the ITGWU (Irish Transport and General Workers' Union), when he told Derry Trades Council: "In the past, the shirt trade was a labour-intensive industry, but because of the introduction of modern production methods, it is now a contraction industry." Statistics from the Ministry of Commerce supported this, as they revealed that the 1955 figure of 7,250 employed in the shirt and collar industry in Derry had fallen to 5,550 by 1966.

Unfortunately this contraction was to increase, with devastating results, beyond any predictions: imports of nylon shirts from Portugal and polyester/cotton shirts from Hong Kong increased significantly. This situation was compounded by the massive 80% increase in freight charges imposed by British Railways on container traffic from the North West and other places outside Belfast going to Britain. All these factors appeared to come to a head in 1967, when most of the factories, both large and small, were working a shorter week except Tillies, whose directors would not concede to the unions' request to operate shorter hours. Instead, Tillie and Henderson introduced redundancy. The only apparent concession from the company was an undertaking to consider representations about individual cases of hardship. They had also agreed, if circumstances permitted, to re-employ workers who had not learned a particular skill during their time in the factory.

The Friday pay-offs were tense times for the girls. They nervously

Shirt manufacturers' chief says —

CHEAP PORTUGUESE SHIRTS MEAN LOSS OF 2,000 DERRY JOBS

COMPETITION from Portuguese shirts that ar[...]
4/11 each is ma[...]
to the Derry shi[...]
irt Manufactur[...]
the week-end.

DERRY FACTORY MAY PAY OFF 120 WORKERS

MORE bad news on [...]
dustrial front for D[...]
this time in the s[...]
dustry.
Proposals for redund[...]
Tillie & Henderson's [...]
one of the largest in t[...]
have been placed befo[...]
officials of the Irish Tr[...]

MORE TALKS ON FACTORY PAY-OFF PROPOSAL

TWO DIRECTORS of the shirt
firm of Tillie & Henderson

New Threat To Derry Shirt Industry

Derry's shirt industry is facing a new fight for survival.
Up until a year ago the rising flood of cheap imports from Hong Kong and other low cost countries of the Far East, threatened to kill the industry. The Board of Trade eventually applied restrictions which gave the industry a new deal.

INCREASED FREIGHT CHARGES : CHEAP IMPORTS

DERRY FACTORIES MAY CLOSE

—SHIRT INDUSTRY CHIEF WARNS

"Large and small will be affected"

A WARNING that increased freight charges coming [...]
on [...]
the impo[...]
end for [...]
has bee[...]
the Shir[...]

Speakin[...]
Derry Cha[...]
Mr Guckl[...]
the fact t[...]
had refer[...]

"MOST SIGNIFICANT IMPROVEMENT IN WORKING CONDITIONS"

DERRY SHIRT WORKERS TO GET GUARANTEED DAY'S PAY

WHEN Derry City's 6,500 shirt factory workers go off this week on their annual fortnight's paid holidays 750 o[...]
the knowledge that [...]
important progress [...]
ditions in their fact[...]

This is the factory of Messrs. Till[...]
& Henderson, Ltd., the largest factor[...]
in Derry, which will make history whe[...]
it carries out the revolutionary chang[...]
of introducing a guaranteed day's pa[...]
for its workers. 'It is probably th[...]
first shirt and collar factory in Grea[...]
Britain and Ireland to do so.
Down the long years that Derry ha[...]
been famous for its shirt manufactur[...]
ing the position has been that, after wor[...]
ing an hour or two in the mornin[...]
and earning only a few shillings, [...]
number of girls in one department o[...]
a factory could be sent home for th[...]
remainder of the day because, perhap[...]
a bottleneck had developed in anothe[...]
department, and there was consequen[...]
no work immediately available fo[...]
these girls. They furthermore cou[...]
not draw any unemployment bene[...]
for that particular day.
Messrs Tillie & Henderson will no[...]
launch the introduction of guarantee[...]
a full day's pay for all entering th[...]
factory each day.
This is one of several improvement[...]
contained in an agreement just con[...]
pleted between Messrs. Tillie & Ha[...]
dersen and the Irish Transport an[...]
General Workers' Union.

Union Statement

The following statement was issue[...]
yesterday afternoon by the Derr[...]
branch of the Union:—
"After several months of negotia[...]

Tillie and Henderson's transfer to Maydown

REDUNDANCY FIGURE CUT AFTER TALKS

MINISTRY'S ASSURANCES TO UNION REPRESENTATIVES

The number of workers who will be redundant when Messrs. Tillie & Hendersons Ltd. transfer their shirt-making operations from their existing factory at Foyle Road, Derry, is 84. The original estimate was 200.

And the Ministry of Commerce has given an assurance that if the operation at Maydown proves viable it will be prepared to [...]

offer further discussion a specific assurance was given by the Ministry that if the operation of Tillie and Henderson's was proven [...]

NEW THREAT TO THE SHIRT INDUSTRY

Imports from Portugal

THE SHIRT INDUSTRY faces a new threat—this time from Portugal—and the Shirt Manufacturers' Federation here has joined with the British Federation in a plea to the British Board of Trade for protection against it.

Mr. Frank Gucklan, chairman of the Six County Federation, said it had been pointed out to the Minister of State at the Board of Trade, Mr. Mallalieu, that in the first four months of 1967, [...]
shirts had been imported into the U.K. from Portugal, compared with 180,000 dozen shirts in the whole of 1966.
"What", said Mr. Gucklan, "means that in the first year of the financial tariffs being enjoyed under the EFTA agreement, Portugal looks capable to reach a serious threat to the shirt industry—more serious even into this country in comparison with the Hong Kong threat."
"We pointed out to the Minister that the tremendous threat was causing deep concern to the manufacturers of the United Kingdom, and we emphasised that if it was allowed to grow at this rate it was going to become a serious threat to the trade industry—this country's trade in the Hong Kong threat."
Referring to evidence that had been submitted to the Minister and the Minister was sticking a single import entry into cotton and the imports price was to be as against [...]

approximately 15 per cent shirt for home production—the actual cost to the factory to manufacture.
Mr. Gucklan said that according to the information that had been collected labour costs in Portugal varied between one-quarter and one-seventh of what was paid in this country.
He added "Manufacturers in the E.E.C. countries have been standing by with plans ready to manufacture shirts and only waiting for the tariffs to go. One country in particular is West Germany."
He pointed out that America still restricted imports of textiles to a ten per cent level, but that in Britain between 35 and 40 per cent were being imported from overseas.
"No industry can stand up to this, particularly when the competition is coming from low-cost countries where the material for each of those nylon shirts, for example, is costing about 4s." he said.
Mr. Gucklan said the deputation had had a good hearing from Mr Mallalieu, who had promised to give careful consideration to the representations, and to make representations with the federations at the earliest possible moment.

---

opened their pay packets and as one expressed the uncertainty: "You knew there were pay-offs, but you didn't know until you got your pay packet if it was going to be you."

However, local management did exercise some consideration when it came to selecting who would be paid off and who would not, particularly when some entire families of mothers and daughters were working in Tillies. Eithne Duffy remembers the experience: "I was going out that Friday, and Bobby Sherrard stopped to ask me was I paid off; I told him I was. Then he asked about my other two sisters, and when I told him they were also paid off, he told me to ignore the 'note' and come in again on Monday."

A total of 120 women and girls found the note; and in the cutting room, two cutters and four women were told personally that they had to go. At the time, and in the prevailing circumstances, the situation could have been more serious for Tillies' workers. In February 1967, the management of the large Star Factory (also on Foyle Road) surprisingly announced over the Tannoy system at the lunch break to the workforce of 280 women and girls that the factory was to close the following month. What made all these pay-offs more tragic was that some of the husbands and brothers of the factory women also lost their jobs with the closure of the Monarch Electric Factory at Bligh's Lane.

Factory closure was to become one of the major causes of the unemployment blight in the city; it appeared that the whole structure of the shirt industry in Derry was seriously weakening. Equally worrying for the remaining women working in Tillies was the discovery that the very structure of the building they were in was also weakening. At least, that was the reason given by Tillies' directors in Chester to the unions and the press in a shock announcement five years later, in November 1972, which stated that the Foyle Road factory was to close and re-locate to Maydown Industrial Estate on the outskirts of the city. The announcement said:

> The company's present premises at Foyle Road are in urgent need of repairs, which, in its present state of economic circumstance,

the firm could not undertake, and propose to transfer to a smaller factory at Maydown, with a small workforce of some 230 workers compared with the existing workforce of 480.

It was believed at the time among the workers that the real reason for the move was that the five-storey antiquated Victorian building on Foyle Road was seen as totally unsuited to modern production techniques. The smaller ground-floor Maydown premises were more suitable for TSE to achieve its potential of a smaller, more efficient and economic production unit, which was why it was introduced into Tillies in the first instance. The decision to relocate came at a time when the competition of the cheap foreign shirt was having a disastrous effect in the city, with the closure of the large Wilkinson's Strand Road shirt factory and Littles' Distillery Brae factory. Also, the very successful Ben Sherman factory on Abercorn Road beside Tillies was soon to lose government funding. Moving to Maydown with a

OLD DERRY SHIRT CONCERN WILL CLOSE TODAY

Tillie and Henderson's shirt factory at the Maydown industrial estate, near Derry will close down today. Its closure will end a 130-year link with the city.

The company, which previously had premises at Bridge, employed over 1,000 people, but in recent years it has suffered the same economic setbacks as other textile manufacturing factories and in November, 1972, it closed its factory in the city and moved to Maydown.

Derry received a shock in December last when the company announced that 240 of the 290 workers there would lose their jobs. Despite efforts by the I.T. & G.W.U., these lay-offs took place.

The company's factory in the Co. Donegal town of Carndonagh has also experienced difficulties and seven weeks ago it was announced that it would be closing down.

So far 85 of the 190 work force there have been paid off but the Carndonagh Industrial Action Committee, formed in an attempt to save the Carndonagh operation, has being trying to form a private company.

The official receiver is in Carndonagh and is at present trying to sell the factory there as a going concern.

No date has been set for the closure of the factory but if efforts by the Industrial Action Committee are unsuccessful a date between the end of May and the middle of June is likely.

Mr. Seamus Quinn, Derry branch secretary of the I.T. and G.W.U., told a "Journal" reporter that he had received a telegram from the company chairman, Mr. David Fawsett, telling him of the expected that 86 per cent of company's talks with the Department.

Saying that this was not good enough, Mr. Quinn added: — I am willing to take a deputation of the factory workers to Belfast to see Mr. Stanley Orme if he is willing to have a meeting. I and the union feel we must be a party to any negotiations and we must be in on any such negotiations between the Department of Commerce and the company."

It is understood that the Department of Commerce is examining this company's present position to see if a new product can be made which will enable the company to re-employ its former workers or, failing that, to attempt to find a new tenant for the factory.

IMPORTS BLAMED

A spokesman for Tillie & Henderson told a "Journal" reporter yesterday that the

Factory Jobs Shock: Orme Asked To Meet Workers

Talks are going on between the Department of Commerce and the Tillie and Henderson company following the shock announcement by the company that 240 of the 290 workers in their Maydown, Derry, factory are to lose their jobs.

"But this is not good enough," an Irish Transport and General Workers' Union spokesman said last night. "We are seeking a meeting with the company chairman."

And the spokesman for the company's headquarters in Chester, warned: "It is expected that 86 per cent of the shirts sold in the U.K. next year will be imports. Add this to the fact that a new agreement has been made with polyester cotton shirt manufacturers in Hong Kong and the position is bound to worsen."

He added: — "The shirts from Hong Kong and the Far East are made of polyester cotton, which is rapidly replacing nylon warp-knit material. The Maydown factory manufactured the almost unwanted nylon shirts for the U.K. market and had a contract with Marks and Spencers. However, Marks and Spencer were forced to cut back on their own buying contracts.

SHOCK

The announcement of the Maydown factory pay-offs came as a severe shock in Derry. It took industry and trade unions by surprise. First intimation of the pay-offs was given to Mr. Seamus Quinn,

branch secretary of the Irish Transport and General Workers' Union, who immediately despatched telegrams to Mr. Stanley Orme, Minister of State, and to the company's headquarters in Chester.

Mr. Quinn told Mr. Orme his shock at the sudden rundown at the factory, one of the oldest and most firmly established shirt factories in the area.

"The rundown, with the loss of 240 jobs, is a cruel blow to the city," Mr. Quinn said. "Request your immediate intervention."

MEETING REQUESTED

In his telegram to the company's headquarters Mr. Quinn said: "Generations of Derry workers served this company loyally for many years. I am dismayed that such a decision should be taken without any prior consultation with the workers' representatives. Request immediate meeting to explore the situation."

Tillie & Henderson's began trading in the late 1830s before transferring to Derry more than 100 years ago. It has been a supplier to Marks & Spencer for more than fifty years. In 1972, with Department of Commerce assistance, Tillie & Henderson was relocated in a modern State built factory at smaller and more efficient operation was very much a case of survival, for it was obvious from the statement to the press that Tillies had grave financial difficulties.

No longer would Tillies' factory horn be heard. The familiar sight of crowds of women and young girls going up and down Tillies' iron steps and across the parquet walkway to the alternative entrance would be seen no more. Tillies' workforce, with the exception of a well-depleted cutting staff, could now be seen boarding the bus at Foyle Street for Maydown. The reason why the cutting staff remained in the Foyle Road building and kept it open was because the government factory at Maydown was so small. It could not incorporate a cutting room; so the Ministry of Commerce reacted by promising to erect a prefabricated building for that purpose. In the meantime, the cutwork from Foyle Road was transported on a daily basis to Maydown. It was not until the spring of 1974 that the cutting operation also moved to Maydown. So, the doors of Tillie and Henderson shirt factory building, which had admitted generations of Derry women and girls through them, were finally closed and chained after one hundred and eighteen years.

At the time of Tillies moving to Maydown, the Minister of Commerce gave a specific assurance that if the operation at Maydown was proven viable, and should a suitable site become available in the city, then a new factory would be built on the west bank of the Foyle. It was a promise that he would not be called upon to fulfil, for the final episode of the Tillie and Henderson story was about to end abruptly in 1976 when Brian Nolan was summoned to Chester and told to cease operations at Maydown.

It was speculated, at the time, that the cause of closure resulted from the problem of excess capitalisation and productivity. This, basically translated, meant that too much money had been spent on buying too much new machinery making too many nylon shirts that were too much out of fashion. The situation was made all the more serious because Marks and Spencer were not 'drawing off' orders quickly enough. Consequently, Tillies' cash-flow trickled to a stop. The end had come for this historic building. It shut its doors to the factory girls and the world for the last time.

Epilogue

The Tillie and Henderson story could be seen as an epitaph to shirt making in Derry and to the spirit of the women, girls and the small number of men who sustained it as a major industry. At the centre of the city's economy, the shirt industry was to Derry what the coal industry had been to the mining towns, cities and villages of England and Wales. It was a way of life as much as a way of earning a living. The young female school-leavers followed their mothers, elder sisters and extended family into the factories, and their earnings sustained the family in a city plagued with male unemployment.

The traditional linked arms of the women going to the factories was symbolic of the closeness and companionship within the shirt-factory culture, which provided for the social, economic and emotional needs of the girls.

Any personal problems could be discussed in heart-to-heart talks in the smoking parlours, also seen among the girls as communication centres, and the various business agreements were strictly controlled by the 'pay-up-on-Friday' code.

The companionship on the speed belt, where singing was infectious, was greatly weakened by the divisive and disruptive elements of time-study production. This system changed the whole working atmosphere within the factory, affecting working relationships and creating competition among the girls to chase the extra money. The singing, sewing girl on the speed belt gradually became the competitive, isolated and captive worker of Time Study Engineering.

The sound of the factory horn, which in many respects was the city's alarm clock, can be heard no more. The entire shirt industry of Derry, with the exception of one medium-sized and two smaller factories, has all but disappeared under foreign competition. The shirt factories are history now and written into the folklore of the older generation.

I feel privileged to have been part of that history as a shirt cutter in Tillies, working with the factory girls for twenty-two years. And the city owes them a great debt of admiration and gratitude. Sadly, the building that could and should have stood as a permanent monument to the women and girls who worked under its roof has now become historical debris. Hopefully, this publication will stand to acknowledge those workers and to recognise the immense contribution of the Derry factory girls to the social and economic life of the city as they sewed, sang, sweated, laughed and cried in all Derry's factories.

Tillie's Brae as the factory lies dormant.

Snapshots of Life in Maydown

All photographs courtesy of Margaret and Rose O'Kane
unless otherwise attributed.

Lunch break at Maydown. (L/R): Patsy McIntyre, Unknown, Tillie
O'Donnell (standing) and Unknown.

Listening to music. Left, (L/R): Bernadette Moore, Philomena Duddy and
Stella Houston. Right, Bridget Rodden, a collar worker.

Retirement presentation at Maydown. (L/R): Sammy Moore (cutting-room manager), Margaret Heywood (Miss Tillies, 1975), Brian Nolan (director of Tillies Éire Ltd), Charlie Cauley (recipient and lay planner), Rosetta Cauley, Jim Stainthorpe (deputy factory manager) and Margaret Mulheron (personnel manager). (Courtesy Sheila Molloy)

132

Happy workers at Maydown. (L/R): Vera McConnell, Isobel Moore, Paddy Morrison, Margaret O'Kane and Una McShane.

133

Mugs at the ready. (L/R): Eileen McDaid, Lily Murray, Pat McKeegan and Unknown.

Taking it easy.

A wall line-up. (L/R): Unknown, Margaret O'Kane, Peggy James, Rose O'Kane, Unknown and Eilish McLaughlin.

Hair pulling. (L/R): Eilish McLaughlin, Unknown, Kitty Gallagher, Patsy McIntyre and Unknown.

Camera capers. (L/R): Peggy O'Neill, Margaret O'Kane (supervisor), Seamus Mullan (cutter) and Peggy James.

All smiles at Maydown.

Hold for the camera. (L/R): Seamus Mullan (cutter) holds Rose O'Kane and Peggy James holds Sammy Moore (cutting-department manager).

New uniforms. Standing (L/R): Mary Harkin and Nora Cradden. Sitting (L/R): Tessa Gallagher and Lily Gurley.

Maydown dinner dance in the Golden Slipper, Magilligan, Autumn 1975.

Keeping busy at Maydown. (Courtesy Brian Nolan and Patrick Hegarty)

137

No looking at the camera at Maydown. (Courtesy Brian Nolan and Patrick Hegarty)

The folders at work at Maydown. (Courtesy Brian Nolan and Patrick Hegarty)

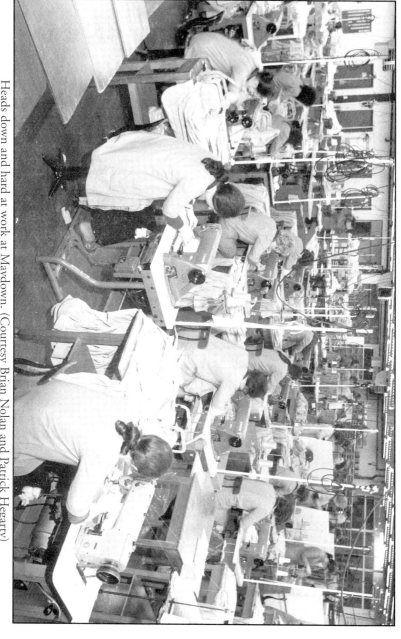

Heads down and hard at work at Maydown. (Courtesy Brian Nolan and Patrick Hegarty)

140

An evening of reminiscence in 2004. Sitting (L/R): Mary Hegarty (née McAllister), Stella McDaid, Bridie McCormick (née McGurk) and Patsy Durnin. Standing (L/R): Berna McDermott (née McShane), Kitty Duffy, Eithne Glackin (née Duffy), Margaret McDaid (née Long, USA) and Maisie Moore (née McLaughlin). (Courtesy Patsy Durnin)

141

Factory Demolished

Demolition begins on the factory, January 2003. (Courtesy Hugh Gallagher)

Tumbled remains on Tillie's Brae. (Courtesy Hugh Gallagher)

Demolition reveals an old mural, copied from an engraving depicting a view of the city from the Waterside in the 1840s.

Tillie's Brae without Tillies. (Courtesy Bobby White)

Nothing left standing but the factory gates. (Courtesy Bobby White)